PASSPORT

TO PROSPERITY

*Exposing and Eradicating
the Devils Behind Poverty*

PASSPORT

TO PROSPERITY

*Exposing and Eradicating
the Devils Behind Poverty*

by Tiffany Buckner
Anointed Fire™ House

**Passport to Prosperity
Exposing and Eradicating the Devils Behind
Poverty**
Copyright © 2016
Author: Tiffany Buckner
Email: info@anointedfire.com

Publisher: Anointed Fire™ House
www.anointedfirehouse.com

Anointed Fire
ISBN-13: 978-0692649008
ISBN-10: 069264900X

Disclaimer: This book is designed to provide
information and motivation to our readers. It is sold
with the understanding that the publisher is not
engaged to render any type of psychological, legal,

<u>Dedication</u>

*I dedicate this book to my Savior and
Deliverer: Jesus the Christ.*

Table of Contents

Introduction

The system of this world is an ungodly system designed to pervert God's people and rob them of their inheritance. For this reason, poverty is more common than prosperity. At the same time, religious traditions and lack of knowledge have kept many in the church bound. It was never God's intention for His people to be broke, busted and disgusted. It was never God's intention for His people to be distracted by bills that they cannot manage. After all, He called us to be the heads and not the tails; we are the lenders and not the borrowers. We should come behind in no good thing. How is it then that many in the church have fallen into the same financial pits that the world has fallen into? It's simple: The church keeps following the world!

Nowadays, many of the scriptures we frequently quote are nothing more to us than mere words that we chant in hopes of moving heaven. In other words, we have not allowed those words to penetrate our hearts. For this reason, many in the church are not experiencing the manifestations of what they claim they are believing God for. The average believer does not approach YAHWEH as if He is the living God; they approach Him the same way they approach the tombs of their loved ones! In other words, many in today's church have come to believe that God no longer exists, and this is not true!

In *Passport to Prosperity*, you will learn about the stronghold of poverty and how the enemy systematically binds believers with it. This comprehensive guide to wealth will help you to understand how Satan gets rights to your finances as well as how to evict him from your life and your bank account once and for all! This powerful book is a combination of practical teaching, in-depth knowledge and demonology.

Your Relationship with Money

Every human being alive is in several relationships. Some of those relationships are good, and some of those relationships are not-so-good. We have relationships with our family members, friends, co-workers, church family and the list goes on. In addition to our relationships with people, we have relationships with inanimate objects such as food, money, medicine, etc. And just like people, we can have unhealthy relationships with objects as well.

Every relationship we have is a fertile relationship that will birth something in our lives. Our godly relationships produce godly results, whereas, our ungodly relationships produce ungodly results. For example, a godly relationship with a relative will always draw you closer to God. This simply means that God is serving as the head of that relationship, and the evidence of God being in that relationship will be the blessings that are produced from it. An ungodly relationship with a family member, however, will always produce chaos, setbacks, unforgiveness, strife and so on. This means that God is not a part of that connection, and because He's not in it, it will be full of turmoil. A healthy (godly) relationship with food will keep your body nurtured, energized and healthy, whereas, an unhealthy (ungodly) relationship with food will keep your body starved of the nutrients it needs to survive. When this happens, your metabolism can slow down, thus, causing you to become sluggish and unhealthy. The same goes for money.

We all have a relationship with money. We will always know how good our relationship with money is based on its proximity to us. When we don't have the wisdom, knowledge and understanding we need to attract wealth to ourselves, our relationship with money will be estranged. In such cases, we'll become like scorned lovers. We'll stalk money, work harder than necessary to get it, and even worse, we will begin to love money. One rule we must always operate in is: Never love anything that cannot love you back, otherwise, the relationship will become one-sided.

1 Timothy 6:10 (KJV): For the love of money is the root of all evil: which while some coveted after, they have erred from the faith, and pierced themselves through with many sorrows.

We were made in YAHWEH'S image, and as such, we have His very nature. He is our Creator, and therefore, we are creative. That's why we are called creatures, or better yet, God's creations. To create means to form something. God formed man from the dust of the ground, and He formed woman from a man's rib. We have the ability to form things, even though whatever we form does not have life. *Note: We don't form children; God does.*

We have to loan our lives to whatever we form with our hands. For example, a house will deteriorate when no one is living in it. When a person lives in that house, the humidity in it is kept under control. This stops the house from deteriorating as quickly. In a sense, we loan our lives to wherever we live because we turn on the lights, turn off the lights, clean the place, kill any mold or mildew we see, and so on. We come into an unoccupied dwelling (house) and occupy it.

Because we are creative beings, our purpose is to create things, and of course, whatever we create must be God-approved. We shouldn't create anything that repels souls from Christ; all of our creations are supposed to draw souls to Him or to glorify Him. Nevertheless, we have an enemy who encourages us to do the opposite of what God created us to do. That's because Satan understands that a creature that is not creative is like the fig tree that Jesus cursed because it produced no fruit. It was a fig tree, so it was supposed to produce figs. Satan also understands that he can use our creative abilities for his own kingdom, and that's why he likes to pervert the hearts of God's people. A singer is created to sing for the Lord; that is the singer's assignment. However, a singer perverted by sin will sing songs that promote Satan's doctrine of lies. The point is... our ability to attract wealth is within us; it is tied to our creative abilities. When we don't tap into our creative abilities, we won't operate as we are designed to do, and this leads to unfulfilled expectations, depression, marital problems and poverty. It also leads to us prostituting our gifts to the enemy.

Wealth is attracted to creativity, whether that creativity is used in a good way or a bad way. Of course, God places the wealth in the hands of the righteous, but Satan teaches the unrighteous to tap into their abilities to create things. By doing this, he teaches them to tap into the wealth that's locked up within them, and then, he uses that wealth to build his dark kingdom. He teaches them to love money, which causes them to fall under the witchcraft of idolatry. When this happens, they set themselves up to fall into the many snares set by the enemy and that snare is.... to enter an ungodly relationship with money.

God has already spoken to the wealth of the earth, and it must obey Him. Even though it may vacation in the homes and bank accounts of the unrighteous, wealth will always find its way back into the possession of the righteous.
Proverbs 13:22 (ESV): A good man leaves

an inheritance to his children's children, but
the sinner's wealth is laid up for the
righteous.
Psalms 112:1-3 (ESV): Blessed is the man
who fears the Lord, who greatly delights in
his commandments! His offspring will be
mighty in the land; the generation of the
upright will be blessed. Wealth and riches
are in his house, and his righteousness
endures forever.

There are three ways that a person can have
an ungodly relationship with money.
1. **They can pursue it.** Money is not
   designed to be pursued; it is
   designed to pursue the righteous.
   Anytime a person pursues money,
   they are operating against their own
   creative designs.
2. **They can repel it.** Lack of
   knowledge repels money. Sin repels
   wealth. Slothfulness repels wealth.
3. **They can withhold it.** Believe it or

not, money is a seed. It was never designed to be withheld. Wealth is our ability to sow into the creative abilities of others so that we can reap a harvest from them, and vice versa. This is also called trading in the natural world.

An ungodly relationship with money causes money to become the sower and the person who was supposed to sow it becomes the thing that is sowed. They become the seed, working tirelessly to earn more money until they find themselves prematurely resting in the ground. This undoubtedly is a perverted or godless relationship that produces nothing but death. The presence of chaos in a relationship, whether it be a relationship with a person or a relationship with an inanimate object oftentimes signals that God is absent from that union.

We have to be very careful in our dealings with money because the love of money isn't just a feeling; it's a heart condition. The love of money is like cancer to one's soul. Like a drug addiction, it starts off with someone entertaining a series of thoughts that they should have cast down. Eventually, those thoughts grow into fantasies, meaning, they are no longer just ideas that the person is mentally visiting. Instead, they have become the desires of that person's heart. When a desire rises up in a person's heart, that desire causes the heart to send up a firestorm of imaginations. Because we are creatures (creative beings), we will begin to mentally create ways in which we can have whatever it is that we've been imagining. After that, we will try to physically recreate the events we saw in our mind. If our hearts are good, we will think of good ways to get whatever it is that we want. If our hearts are evil, we will think of wicked things to do to get what we want. It goes without saying that even if the heart is good, our attempts to manipulate our realities and cause them to fit our imaginations can produce bad results. This is similar to conception, whereas, during sex, a man releases sperm and that sperm swims through a woman's vagina, into her uterus, and eventually makes its way to her Fallopian tubes. The surviving sperm will cluster on top of the egg, but only one of the estimated two hundred and fifty million sperm released will fertilize the egg. After fertilization, the egg's outer layer thickens to prevent any other sperm from entering it. The fertilized egg then goes through a series where it divides into many cells as it makes its way to the uterus, where it implants itself. The fertilized egg will remain in its mother's uterus for nine months until the baby is fully formed and able to survive on his or her own. The love of money starts off the same way, but always ends differently. The person who the enemy is trying to bind is first entertained by an idea, and that idea becomes an imagination. If that imagination is not cast down, it will make its way into the person's heart where it will implant itself as a belief, desire or a plan. From there, the person is bound and will start to have symptoms of their new heart condition. Those symptoms can be anything from anxiousness to the sudden intolerance of anyone they feel is a threat to their new plans.

The love of money will eventually birth a wrongful relationship with it, whereas, the people bound will use their creative abilities to get wealth. Nevertheless, the average person will not form the creations that God has planted in their hearts to form. Instead, they will lie, manipulate and cheat to get whatever it is that they want. Some people will start overworking themselves, while others will begin to wrestle with procrastination. Procrastination occurs when a person has a vision but puts that vision off to do something else. Oftentimes, procrastination is the result of intimidation. Some people are simply intimidated by their own visions, so they file them away in their hearts, hoping to revisit them when they feel they are financially or spiritually ready for them. For example, as a business owner and coach, I've spoken with many people about starting their own businesses, but it was hard to reach them because they had wrongful relationships with money. Their excuses are almost always the same: I need to earn the money first, so I'm going to work here (their jobs) for ___ more years and once I get my money together, I'm going to start my business. Of course, in most cases, that business never gets started, or at least, by them. Years pass and most people who have not started their businesses begin to see their unfulfilled visions as childish fantasies that were overridden by the challenges (and bills) that came with adulthood. This isn't true. They were simply bound by the love of money and that love of money was overwhelmed by their lack of knowledge.

A wrongful relationship with money has led many God-fearing saints outside of the love, fear and admonition of God and set their feet on a path to everlasting destruction. The problem here is... we all know what money can do for us. Just about every problem we have can be fixed with the right amount of money. Just about every desire we have can be fulfilled with the right amount of money. Truthfully, for a person who has never been wealthy, it's hard to imagine how a wealthy person could ever be burdened by anything. Nevertheless, a wealthy man suffers the same amount of heartache that a poor man suffers, but he has a different set of problems. For the wealthy man, it's hard to find someone who can relate to him because he has to guard his wealth and his family from people who love money and would do anything to get their hands on it. There are a lot of poisonous people hanging out at wealthy gatherings, and many of them are wealthy themselves. The issue isn't that they need money. The issue is that they have become greedy and are always on the prowl for opportunities to steal or manipulate other wealthy individuals. Because of this, a wealthy man's circle is a lot smaller than the circle of a poor man. His reality is different. At the same time, a poor man's problem can be that he has plenty of people who can relate to where he is and not enough people who can relate to where he wants to be. How is this a problem? Think about it this way. If you were an alcoholic trying to stop drinking, would it benefit you that everyone around you is an alcoholic? No. You would need someone who has beaten the addiction to alcohol; that way, that person can show you how to get free and help you to understand that you can be free. A poor man can call all of his friends when he is unable to pay a bill, but in most of those cases, none of them are able to help him. They can only offer him words of encouragement. However, should one of his friends loan the money to him, that friendship would automatically be tested and strained. How so? More than likely, the borrower has a problem with paying off what he owes. When the time comes for him to repay his friend, he will likely measure his financial situation against his friend's financial situation. If he feels that his friend is better off than he is, he will not want to repay him or he will want to pay him back on his own terms and in his own timing. This would leave the lender feeling used and unappreciated, and of course, put a strain on their relationship. Keep in mind that the man bound by poverty has a wrongful relationship with money, and because of this, he has damaged many relationships in his attempt to get the one thing he loves the most: money. Of course, such behavior is demonic and it opens the door for the enemy to attack that man's finances.

When I was eight years old, I can remember a few of my relatives reaching out to my parents to ask for money. Of course, they used the term "borrow", but even in my young age, I knew that the word "borrow" was code for "give." Because of this, I would often try to reason with my parents, begging them not to loan out the money because they weren't going to get it back. We were poor enough as it was. Anytime my parents agreed to loan out money, it was money set aside for a bill. Of course, when that money wasn't paid back, they had to either put the bills off or let the utilities go off. I knew that if they "loaned" the money out, a series of familiar events would take place that would leave my parents frustrated for weeks on end.

1. After receiving the loan, my relatives would joyfully thank my parents, declaring to them how much they appreciated them. They'd tell my parents of the impending doom that they saved them from, and then, go on to proclaim their love for them. Believe it or not, to a person with a wrongful relationship with money, this *is* their way of paying back the borrower... by complimenting him or her.

2. As the days passed by, they would give my parents a bunch of unsolicited information about sudden bills or expenses they had. Of course, they wouldn't ask for an extension, nor would they mention the money they owed my parents; this would be

their way of saying, "I will not be paying you back this payday."

3. Everything would remain normal at first, but then, as the days towards the borrowers' payday drew nearer, their attitudes would begin to sour and they'd come around less and call less.

4. Payday arrives and they (the borrowers) were nowhere to be found. Even when their cars were in their driveways, no one would answer the door.

5. My parents would call repeatedly but get no answer.

6. After a few days or a week of avoiding my parents' calls, the elusive borrowers would call them back and berate them for calling them so much. They'd then remind them of the "situation" they were in and the story they'd given them days earlier.

7. Once my parents made it very clear

that they needed their money, my relatives would loudly and grudgingly proclaim to them that they were going to get their money back.

8. The relationship between my parents and those relatives would end temporarily. My parents would never see the money they'd loaned out and the relatives would wait for about six months to a year to start coming around again.

9. The cycle would repeat itself.

People who have wrongful relationships with money will almost always love money more than they love people. That's why most of the people they are in conflict with are people they owe money to. This is also why you should avoid loaning money to someone who has a wrongful relationship with it, unless, of course, you can spare the amount that they are asking for or you simply want to "buy them out of your life."

To "buy someone out of your life" is to simply loan money to someone you know is not going to want to pay you back because of their wrongful relationship with it. In this, you simply loan them the money, and then, do as you would do with anyone else: ask for your money back. When they make excuses, tell them why you need your money back and when you need it back. For a person bound by poverty, this behavior is offensive because whatever money they get in their hands is mentally set aside by them to pay their own bills and entertain themselves. In other words, they are selfish creatures and this is not surprising, given that having a wrongful relationship with money is a selfish act. The borrower would more than likely keep their distance from you because they don't want to pay you back and they are offended by the fact that you asked them to repay you. People who have wrongful relationships with money treat their loved ones the same way they treat bill collectors: they avoid them, berate them and threaten them.

As you've probably noticed, I speak of the terms "poverty" and "having a wrongful relationship with money" collectively. That's because they are one and the same. Poverty isn't just an outward reality; it is mental bondage manifested as an outward reality.

But what about children born into poverty? They are simply children born into the realities that their parents, grandparents, ancestors or their governments created for them. If the government of a land is wicked, the land will suffer. All the same, anytime a person has power over another person, the leader's reality will become the follower's reality.

Proverbs 29:2 (NLT): When the godly are in authority, the people rejoice. But when the wicked are in power, they groan.

Having a wrongful relationship with money is having a demonic relationship with money. Again, you should never love anything that does not have the power or the intelligence to love you back. If you do, the relationship will be unequally yoked, and you'll end up putting more into it than you're getting out of it. People who love money work harder for it and get less than the people who simply love serving God and tapping into the creative gifts He has placed in them. When you tap into your creativity, you tap into the heart of the Creator and that's where you'll find your wealthy place.

How Demons Get Legal Rights

Think back to a relationship you were once in. When you were a part of that relationship, more than likely, you worked hard to ensure that it would survive the tests of time. You apologized when you did nothing wrong and you made the necessary sacrifices to keep that relationship afloat. That was up until the day you realized that the relationship wasn't going anywhere. Instead, it was taking you to some pretty dark places and it had become pretty taxing on you, so just like any good investor, you knew when to cut your losses. Nevertheless, that didn't stop the pain and the disappointment that followed the breakup. Even though you knew that God had someone out there who was better suited for you, you couldn't help but find yourself feeling like you'd been robbed. Eventually, you got over that relationship and moved on with your life. Why did you move on? Because you learned to adapt to a new reality.

Believe it or not, when you are bound by the spirit of poverty, you are in a dysfunctional relationship with that spirit. Sure, it's not a healthy relationship, but like most people in soul ties, you've learned to adapt to the relationship because somehow, you've found something in it that you believe benefits you or will benefit you eventually.

Human relationships rarely last a lifetime, but spiritual relationships (relationships between spiritual beings) often last hundreds, if not, thousands of years. In other words, relationships between demonic spirits and the families they are attached to can last hundreds or thousands of generations. That's because each human being has flesh, a soul and a spirit. When demons attach themselves to human beings, they cannot attach themselves to the spirit of a human being, so they access the soul of the person. Nevertheless, because spirits are eternal beings, they will outlive the soul of a man, and of course, when we die, our spirits leave the realm of the earth. What's left is whatever or whomever we've left behind. Our life is found in our blood, and our blood is the fuel of our souls. Without it, we cannot move, operate or survive. Nevertheless, our blood is passed on to our children and our children's children, and this is how demons pass through one generation to the next generation.

A man's flesh is the outer covering that gives him the license to live in the realm of the earth. It simply indicates that he is authorized to not only walk the face of the earth, but because he is made in the image of God, he has dominion over every living thing in the realm of the earth, including spirits. It goes without saying that it is illegal for a spirit to walk in the earth's realm without a body, and for this very reason, demonic spirits try to legalize their presence by possessing the bodies of human beings.

A man's soul is comprised of his mind, will and emotions. It's the part of the human being that drives him. It's also the place demons like to seat themselves because a man's soul is similar to a vehicle. Whoever is behind the wheel (will) is the one who determines what direction that vehicle (or person) will go in.

The mind referenced here is the conscious mind. The conscious mind controls what we are presently aware of and it is affected by what we see or perceive at any given time. It is also affected by our imaginations. Even though demons like to access the conscious mind, they are more interested in possessing or influencing the subconscious mind, or better yet, the heart of a person.

Our will is like our very own pilot cabins, and we are our very own pilots, of course. What we believe determines the direction we go in each and everyday.
In our pilot cabins, there is also another seat that we commonly refer to as the co-pilot's seat. It goes without saying that when we get saved, we are supposed to get into the co-pilot's seat and let the Holy Spirit be the pilot of our lives, but when we don't trust God, we won't give up our seats to Him.

The average Christian has placed their emotions and the spirit of fear in the co-pilot's seat. God, to them, is nothing more than a mere passenger on this journey they call life. Nevertheless, He happens to be that passenger who has a pilot's license. He is someone they want the ability to call on should the pilot and the co-pilot fall asleep behind the "will" of their lives. It goes without saying, however, that if God is not the pilot, He won't get on the plane.

Our will is pretty much our pilot's respective cockpit controls. It isn't what controls us; it is our God-given ability to behave like God and make a decision on our own. We get to decide who we let into the cockpit of our lives, and we get to decide who drives the plane. Our belief systems, better known as our subconscious minds, are the seats we sit on or the seats we give up.

Our emotions are driven by several forces. They can be external stimulants such as cigarettes, alcohol or drugs. They are also driven by internal stimulants such as adrenaline, soul ties, generational thinking, lack of knowledge and misguided perceptions.

External stimulants are similar to decoy pilots. These pilots are lifeless, plus, they have no license and no real abilities. When we hand our will over to drugs and/or alcohol, we are simultaneously handing the wheels of our lives over to demons. In a sense, we become too intoxicated to navigate our own lives and make sound decisions, so we give up our seats to demonic entities. We do this hoping that they'll steer us to our destination or sedate us to the point where we won't feel the full impact of the foreseeable and unavoidable crash landings we have come to expect.

Another external stimulant is the spirit of fear itself. Fear hijacks the life of an emotional person and steers him or her towards destruction. Fear has the legal right to attack individuals when they are attempting to navigate their own lives because of their lack of faith. It doesn't remove them from the pilot's seat. Oftentimes, it simply paralyzes them or encourages them to paralyze themselves with external stimulants. After that, it takes over the flight or opens the individual up for other demonic spirits to enter. The purpose of the spirit of fear is to disconnect the believer from God, thus, causing them to open their hearts to devils. We understand that demons can't possess a true believer, but what most people don't understand is that when a demon can't possess an individual, it can and will enter that person's heart if it is not guarded. **Proverbs 4:23 (NLT):** Guard your heart above all else, for it determines the course of your life.

An internal stimulant is basically familiarity. We trust whomever we are familiar with, and that's why generational curses are oftentimes governed, carried out and executed by familiar spirits. It's similar to a pilot allowing a stewardess to fly a plane simply because she's stepped into the control room a few times. She's a stewardess, so she cannot fly a plane, but a desperate pilot would be willing to risk his life and the lives of his passengers if he felt that he could not successfully navigate or land the plane he's in control of and if his co-pilot was somehow incapacitated.

Before each day takes off, we make decisions for ourselves based on fear, faith or obligation. Before making these decisions, we pretty much decide who will be in the pilot's seat, who will be in the co-pilot's seat and who will be a passenger. Another way to put it is: Before making these decisions, we pretty much decide "whose will" will be in the pilot's seat, "whose will" will be in the co-pilot's seat, and "whose will" will be nothing more than a mere casualty if our arranged order doesn't work. Of course, we determine who gets behind the wheel of our lives based on what we believe or perceive. If we trust and believe God, He gets the pilot's seat. If we trust and believe ourselves, we'll jump into the pilot's seat and religiously attempt to make God a co-pilot, a passenger or an air traffic control officer. If we believe Satan's report, we will let our emotions drive us. In doing so, we give Satan the ability to make decisions in regards to our lives. Ironically enough, this gives him the ability and the legal right to bring to pass whatsoever it is that we fear because God did not give us a spirit of fear. This means that the spirit of fear is the governor in Satan's kingdom and it gets to determine the fate of the people in submission to it.

Fear isn't just a spirit; it is a state of mind. Just like demonic spirits are illegal in the realm of the earth, it is illegal for a human being to enter the state of fear because it is not a state set up or governed by God. Of course, we are to fear God, but our fear of God is built into us; it's not something we have to will ourselves to do. Even the most wicked of sinners fear God, whether he (or she) knows it or not. How so? If the presence of God were to visit such a person, he or she would tremble with fear. There is a state called reverence, which is righteous fear, meaning that we believe God, acknowledge His Word to be true and submit ourselves to it. Spiritually speaking, reverence is the respect and admonition we give to God. That's why it is a sin to give reverence to a human being.

How does any of this relate to the spirit of poverty? The answer is simple. You have just learned the makeup of who you are and how the Devil seeks to gain access to every part of you. He takes God at His word and looks for every opportunity that he can get to enter the life, heart and/ or mind of a believer.

1 Peter 5:8 (KJV): Be sober, be vigilant; because your adversary the Devil, as a roaring lion, walketh about, seeking whom he may devour.

Pay attention to the referenced scripture. I want to bring your attention to some of the words and terms listed.

Be Sober- We have always associated the word "sober" with alcohol and/or drugs. A person who is sober, in our understanding, is a person who is not under the influence of alcohol or drugs. Nevertheless, the word "sober" also means to be in one's right mind; the mind in which God gave to him or her. To be sober means to have a sound mind. Anytime you are in subjection to the spirit of fear, you are under the influence of whatever it is or whomever it is that you are fearing. Whenever you are prideful, you are under the influence of what the Bible refers to as a haughty spirit. Whenever you believe false doctrines, you are influenced, or better yet, under the influence of the doctrine in which you have subjected yourself to.

Be Vigilant- *Dictionary.reference.com* defines the word "vigilant" as:

- keenly watchful to detect danger; wary: a vigilant sentry.
- ever awake and alert; sleeplessly watchful.

What God is telling us is to always recognize that we have an enemy and he is always on the prowl. We shouldn't get too complacent in our lives and stop resisting the advances of the enemy as well as fighting off any attacks he may be planning. Even in times of peace, we have to remember that we are at war with Satan and his cohorts. That's why the Bible tells us to pray without ceasing (see 1

Thessalonians 5:17). God isn't saying that we ought to neglect sleep, quit our jobs and pray from sunrise to sunset. He is saying that we should never stop having a prayer life. We should be praying daily, and our daily prayers should not be religious. Instead, they should be intimate. Why is this? Think of it this way. If you keep bolting the front door anytime a thief is in your neighborhood and he notices that you keep bolting the front door, he'll attempt to break in through the back door or a window. When we pray religiously, we keep guarding the same places. The enemy simply finds another area of our lives to attack... areas that we didn't realize needed guarding. Additionally, religious prayers do nothing to build our faith in God. We learn to have faith in our prayers and not the God who answers our prayers.

The Devil, As a Roaring Lion, Walketh About- When and why does a lion roar?

These types of questions are necessary to gain understanding of the scriptures. Lions don't roar when they are around living prey because they'd scare them away. Lions roar to intimidate other lions; they roar to claim their territories, and they roar to get the attention of other lions within their pride. The Bible says that the Devil walks about like a roaring lion, meaning, he's trying to intimidate people. Satan needs you to enter the state of fear because it's under his government, and it is there that he has legal rights to you. His roars also serve as a proclamation to the angels of God that the person or people he is pursuing or attacking belongs to him, or he at least thinks he has the legal right to devour them.

He walks about, meaning, he is always on the move. He is a resilient force of evil because he has nothing left to lose.

Seeking Whom He May Devour- He seeks

"whom" he may devour, which means, Satan cannot devour everyone.

The word "devour" means to eat quickly. It also means to consume or overtake something. If you've ever been under the influence of an attack (not under attack), you can probably relate to the term, "When it rains, it pours." This statement, in layman's terms, means that when one bad thing happens, it normally starts a domino effect of evil. When a person is overwhelmed by an attack, that person is basically in a tug-of-war with the enemy. It's similar to what Satan does with the angels when he roars. He is claiming that the person he is attacking belongs to him; he is saying that he has the legal rights to that person. With us (people), he will try to kill, steal or destroy something in our lives. When this happens, we perceive that we are under an attack, but the truth is, the enemy is simply staking claim to something or someone because of sin, an active generational curse or an unsevered soul tie. If you don't know your rights through the Word of God, you can't effectively fight him off. This means that he will steal something or someone from you simply because you were not armed with a weapon. In other words, you were tested, but you didn't know the Word, so you failed the test. When he attacks a person who he does not have the full legal rights to because that person has repented or that person is currently under the grace (protection) of God, the angels will fight him off. In most cases, we are not "under an attack"; instead, when the enemy tries to consume, or better yet, devour us, we are "under the influence" of an attack. At the same time, if we believe God, we are "under the influence" of the Word of God. We either believe that we are defeated or we believe that Christ has already defeated Satan when He took our sins to the cross with Him.

In relation to poverty, Satan is always trying to get legal rights to our resources since he cannot attack our Source (YAHWEH). If we don't know our rights, we pretty much leave the door unlocked for the enemy.

Satan navigates through a person's finances by getting them to:

Sow into bad ground- When you sow into evil ground, you must remember that the ground itself is governed by Satan. This means he can contaminate the harvest, and/ or he can uproot every seed you've sown. Additionally, some seeds won't take root when planted in the wrong soil. For example, it is difficult, but not impossible, for palm trees to grow in cold climates. If you plant a palm tree in Canada, more than likely, it will never grow because the climate would kill it. However, a skilled horticulturist with the right tools may be able to grow a tree in Canada. The point is... it is not wise to plant seeds in places where you personally have to have the skill to raise them! As believers, we understand that God is the one who gives the increase, so when you sow seeds in bad ground, you have to submit to the law in which Christ delivered you from. You would have to find ways to get that seed to grow up and you'd have to give that seed your undivided attention.

Refuse to sow because of an ungodly (idolatrous) relationship they have with their money- Money is a resource and not a source; it is a seed and not the harvest itself. We've learned to see money as the answer to all of our wants and needs, but God didn't design money to take His place. It was designed for trade, meaning, you give something, and then, you get something in return. If you sow a seed, you'll reap whatever is in that seed if you sow it in good ground and take care of it. When people have an ungodly relationship with their money, it simply means that they have learned to trust in the power they believe that money has. Think about it this way. In 6000 BC, people used cattle and produce as currency. They would often exchange, for example, cattle for services or to pay off fines. Can you imagine what would have happened if a farmer had an ungodly relationship with his cattle, whereas, he refused to sell them because he enjoyed eating them? His wealth would be in the number of cattle that he hadn't eaten yet, but eventually, he would eat himself out of supply.

Doubt God- Doubting God is the same as believing Satan. You either believe God or you believe Satan, and whosoever you believe is the one whose doctrine you are in submission to. God is not the author of confusion, so the doctrine of confusion is authored by Satan. When you doubt God, you become a student in Satan's classroom, and this gives him a teacher's rights to you. He can pass you (which we know he rarely does) or he can fail you. He can give you detention, or better yet, make you stay in a place far longer than you were supposed to be.

Currently, there are more than four thousand religions in this world, but there is only one truth. There are 50 states in the United States of America, but in the spirit realm, there are two states: truth and lies. Understand that our words are spirit, and that's why Jesus is the living Word of God. For this reason, it was impossible for Jesus to have returned to God without having fulfilled His assignment in the realm of the earth. God declared what He would do and the Word became flesh. When the Word became flesh, He moved, thought and behaved in accordance with what God had spoken. If you believe the Word of God, you are in submission to the authority of

God. If you don't believe God, you are in submission to demonic authority. Of course, God is sovereign, which means that every kingdom, king, and authority must bow to Him, but when you submit to a lie, you submit to the governor of the doctrine of lies.

There are reportedly five major world religions, but the truth is... there is one major religion that goes by undetected. It is the largest religion on the face of this earth today and it has many denominations under it. This religion is called confusion. When God said that He is not the author of confusion, He was letting us know that confusion is more than a state of mind; it is a doctrine in itself, whereas, the person in submission to it has a double-mind. They are trying to abide by two or more doctrines, and by doing so, they form their own denomination under the doctrine of confusion. You'll notice, for example, that the religion of Islam has a lot of Christian beliefs, meaning, it is a doctrine of lies, seasoned with truth. It is a denomination under the doctrine of confusion.

Confusion is a war brought on by two or more beliefs. That's why the Word tells us that a double-minded man is unstable in all his ways. He's unstable because he has not settled upon a belief, therefore, he is unpredictable, anxious and without a solid foundation. He's like a man who is being forced to choose between two girlfriends. If he thinks that he loves them both, he loses his peace, good health and finances trying to keep them both.
When you doubt God in the area of your finances, you give Satan rule over them.

Disobey God- To disobey God means that you are aware of the direction He wants you to go in, but you choose to go contrary to His will. The Bible tells us that such an act is called rebellion, and rebellion is as (like) the sin of witchcraft. How is rebellion like witchcraft? God gave us a part of Himself which enables us to access His unlimited power. What did He give us? He gave us a force called "will" and He gave us the freedom to exercise that will. Our will, or ability to move, think and reason is a form of power. As a matter of fact, it is the power that makes us more like God, so anytime we are active, we are operating in and under a power. When we stay in God's will, we are in submission to God, and therefore, we can legally access His power through Christ Jesus. Nevertheless, when we use our abilities to do the opposite of what God gave us permission to do, we are using our power to do evil. This means that we are practicing a form of witchcraft. Witches, sorcerers, and occultists often move things using illegal demonic powers, but a Christian in rebellion uses the power which God has granted him or her to perform a task. This is an abuse of power and a form of perversion. Again, disobedience places you in a dark state, and of course, I'm not just speaking of a state of mind. It places you in a state of existing... a place where Satan exalts himself as the governing authority. Understand this: Whatever state you live in, that is the state you'll have to pay taxes to, and the government of that state gets to determine how much they are going to tax you.

Fear Satan, people or circumstances- Fear of anything or anyone who is not YAHWEH is illegal. Fear is a form of reverence. It is an acknowledgment or a recognition of one's power. When we fear God, we acknowledge His power and recognize His sovereignty. When we fear devils or people, we exalt their abilities over God, and therefore, acknowledge them as all-powerful in a certain area of our lives. This is the very same crime the Syrians committed.

1 Kings 20:23-25 (ESV): And the servants of the king of Syria said to him, "Their gods are gods of the hills, and so they were stronger than we. But let us fight against them in the plain, and surely we shall be stronger than they. And do this: remove the kings, each from his post, and put commanders in their places, and muster an army like the army that you have lost, horse for horse, and chariot for chariot. Then we will fight against them in the plain, and surely we shall be stronger than they." And he listened to their voice and did so.

In the above referenced text, we see that the king of Syria had a few officials who gave him some bad advice. By saying that JEHOVAH (YAHWEH) was king of the hills only, they were limiting His power and identifying some other force as more powerful than Him in certain places. Because of this, God defeated them.

1 Kings 20:28 (ESV): And a man of God came near and said to the king of Israel, "Thus says the Lord, 'Because the Syrians have said, "The Lord is a god of the hills but he is not a god of the valleys," therefore I will give all this great multitude into your hand, and you shall know that I am the Lord.'"

Anytime a person calls himself or herself a Christian, but yet fears Satan, their circumstances or people, that Christian is basically saying that God has no power in that area of their lives. Of course, this causes them to be defeated on both sides because such beliefs give Satan the legal authority to attack them in that area and causes the believer to denounce their blessings. For example, if you believe your landlord has the power to determine whether you get to keep your house or not, you have illegally given your landlord the right to evict you. You are pretty much saying that your landlord (a creature) is more powerful than God (the Creator) when it comes to your house (the creation).

Romans 1:24-25 (ESV): Therefore God gave them up in the lusts of their hearts to impurity, to the dishonoring of their bodies among themselves, because they exchanged the truth about God for a lie and worshiped and served the creature rather than the Creator, who is blessed forever! Amen.

Entertain wrongful connections (including friendships, family relationships and submitting to the wrong church)- Entertaining wrongful connections is more than often a sin of rebellion than it is a sin of ignorance. This translates to believers holding on to other people because of fear, dependency and/or familiarity, despite God's command (or warning) that they should disconnect from them. To understand why God disconnects us from ungodly people, we must first understand connections. Anything you connect to, you validate, but anything you are not connected to does not have your seal or approval. Staying connected to someone means that you are basically vouching for the person God has told you to disconnect from. Of course, such behavior could cause other believers to fall into the very snares that have entrapped you. This places you in a state of rebellion. Please remember that any state outside of God's will is a demonic state that is governed by Satan. When you live in a state, you have to pay taxes to that state and you submit to the authority of that state!

The Mammon Principality

We hear the word "stronghold" often as it relates to Christianity, but most Christians don't know what a stronghold is. That's because we've learned to read the words in the Bible without trying to understand the heart of God. We've learned to read words without attempting to understand them, and because of this, the average Christian has memorized a few scriptures (the words spoken by God), but does not recognize the authority of the Word of God. This means that their relationship with God is as unstable as their relationship with the tooth fairy. To them, God is nothing but a story that's been told... one that they are obligated to embrace as truth without actually believing it. In other words, the average believer doesn't believe; they simply say what they feel they are required to say, do what they feel they are required to do, and then, choose a lifestyle they feel is decent enough to label as a Christian lifestyle.

Merriam-Webster's online dictionary defines the word "stronghold" as:

- an area where most people have the same beliefs, values, etc.: an area dominated by a particular group
- a protected place where the members of a military group stay and can defend themselves against attacks.

A stronghold is basically a comfort zone; it is not necessarily a place of safety, but it's a place where people feel safe. The only stronghold that is truly safe is the will of God.

Proverbs 21:22 (ESV): A wise man scales the city of the mighty and brings down the stronghold in which they trust.

2 Samuel 22:1-4 (ESV): And David spoke to the Lord the words of this song on the day when the Lord delivered him from the hand of all his enemies, and from the hand of Saul. He said,"The Lord is my rock and my fortress and my deliverer, my God, my rock, in whom I take refuge, my shield, and the horn of my salvation, my stronghold and my refuge, my savior; you save me from violence. I call upon the Lord, who is worthy to be praised, and I am saved from my enemies.

Think of the neighborhood you grew up in. What type of mentalities were in that area? What was common in that neighborhood? For example, I grew up in a lot of ghettos and impoverished areas, so what was common in my old neighborhoods were theft, fighting and crime. It was also common to see girls as young as 12 years old pregnant. Even though most of the adults weren't okay with young women having babies, they didn't exactly cringe when they saw a young mother because it was common. The average age of a young mother in the areas where I grew up was 16 years old. That's because every community has its own unrecognized government, laws, language, dialect and cultures. For example, in many of the places I grew up, the governors, or better yet, people who set the tone for how others lived were rap and hip hop artists. The culture of those areas was hip hop. Hip hop is not a genre of music; it is a culture where there are several governors (artists who influence people). Of course, Satan is the president of such a culture. Every few years, a new governor would come on the scene with his (or her) own style of music, and many of the former leaders would lose their places in the hearts of the people who once looked to them for instructions. When Snoop Dog was the principality used to influence the next generation, it was not uncommon to see a bunch of young men dressing, speaking and rapping like him. Most young boys wanted to smoke marijuana and act like the man they'd come to idolize. They wore oversized slacks, grew their hair long and stiffened their necks against any form of authority. When Master P was the principality leading the hip hop movement, many young boys found themselves grunting and trying to speak, sound and behave like him. During this time, a lot of young men wore gold (or silver) grills on their teeth, while others, replaced their teeth with caps or crowns. When Tupac was the principality, a lot of women began to profanely refer to themselves and others as female dogs. Women began to dress more provocatively and the hip-hop community (and its followers) began to split into cliques. Some young men claimed to represent the East Side (New York), while some represented the West Side (California). In every city, community, and neighborhood, young men began to label themselves as representatives of the neighborhoods they lived in or frequented, and they began to form groups designed to keep young men from opposing neighborhoods out. People became more territorial and young women became more promiscuous. Division was at an all-time high, and that division has continued to be encouraged by many of today's hip-hop artists. This is what a stronghold is. It is an area governed by a belief system, dominated by a particular group and it is a place where some people feel safe.

Every stronghold has its own military; for example, in many impoverished areas, you'll notice a lot of young men who refer to themselves as "soldiers". They fight; they kill, and they die trying to defend what they believe to be their turf. In many well-to-do communities, the neighborhood soldiers refer to themselves as "neighborhood watch." Every one of these men (and women) are trying to protect their communities in different ways because of their belief systems, experiences and perceived threats.

When I was a young girl (between 11 or 13 years old), my family and I lived in a crime-ridden neighborhood where fights were commonplace. Nevertheless, regardless of all of the crime going on around us, we felt safe. My parents weren't afraid to let us wander the neighborhood alone and the same went for most of the parents there. We knew who our neighborhood criminals were and we weren't scared of them in the least bit. There was one particular guy who we all called Crazy Warren. The rumor in the community was that Crazy Warren had served time in prison for rape. Even though Warren was a strange individual who loved to stare at young women, we weren't afraid of him when we walked in numbers. We would yell at him for staring at us, but he rarely said a word. Nevertheless, none of us would go anywhere near him when we were alone, and if he followed any of us, we would address him the next time we were in a group setting.

Strongholds also represent mindsets that we feel comfortable or safe in. People who are in mental strongholds only feel comfortable around people who are like themselves. That's because with strongholds, there is a language and a culture involved that no one outside of that stronghold will understand. They may understand some things, but not all. Of course, in the United States, most people speak English, but in many communities, there's a unique dialect in operation that sets that community apart from others. Many of these dialects become national dialects. People from around the world (especially young people) embrace dialects in their attempts to put their generations' stamp on society. Of course, these dialects are introduced to the masses through mass media (movies and music).

It goes without saying that poverty isn't just a condition; it's a mindset. Poverty is a stronghold, or better yet, a mental government that's presided over by the principality of Mammon. What is, or better yet, who is Mammon? It is the principality associated with numbers. Mammon keeps an individual's mind focused on money, and the irony is that most people think that the wealthy and those who seek to be wealthy are the only ones affected by or infected with the spirit of Mammon, but this is not true. The spirit of Mammon is the principality (principal devil or prince) that governs the stronghold of poverty. How is this? An impoverished person's reality is the fact that he or she does not have enough to survive or to survive comfortably. Therefore, that individual's entire thought process is overridden by two things: what that person lacks and what that person needs.

When we were growing up in poverty, my parents argued a lot because there was always a need that was not met, which brought about frustration. My mother oftentimes worked two jobs and my dad would almost always be "between jobs." My mother's primary focus was to fulfill every need that her children had, but my dad had succumbed to an entirely different spirit... one that's often found in areas governed by the spirit of Mammon. My dad had a slothful spirit. He simply did not want to work, nor did he want the pressures of responsibility. He wanted money, of course, but he wanted to find an easy, quick way to get rich. This means that he was still under the direction and government of the spirit of Mammon but chose to pursue money outside of the traditional workplace. He was an idea man, so he believed that one of his great ideas would take off someday, and he would be rich. Of course, there was another spirit in operation that assured that this would never happen. It was the spirit of procrastination. Procrastination is broken up into three words: pro, crass, nation.

Pro- Short for the word professional.

Crass- (definition taken from *Merriam-Webster's online dictionary*): (1). having or showing no understanding of what is proper or acceptable, (2). being beneath one's dignity, and (3). guided by or indicative of base or materialistic values.

Tin- (adjective) (definition taken from reference.com): false; worthless; counterfeit.

Nation- (definition taken from *Merriam-Webster's online dictionary*): a large area of land that is controlled by its own government.

What then is a procrastinator? A procrastinator, in short, is a person who has no understanding; a person who operates beneath his or her own ability. By not tapping into the call on their lives, procrastinators do not tap into the value of their lives, making their lives worthless. Additionally, people who don't operate in their own callings often mimic or impersonate other people. In other words, they operate under a spirit of falsehood, or better yet, as counterfeits.

Procrastinators live for the now and not the later. They are guided by their "right now" needs, rather than their future needs. A procrastinator has a reality or mental government that is all his (or her) own. It goes without saying that a procrastinator is subject to the spirit of poverty, and therefore, a citizen under Mammon's government. Procrastinators are not faithful citizens of Mammon, however, because they have a limited vision of their potential, plus, they lack the wisdom, knowledge and understanding to bring their visions to pass. When a person has a vision, but has no understanding, and therefore, no drive to bring that vision to pass, that person will often find himself or herself in depression. Depression is a state of mind; it is the spiritual equivalent of solitary confinement. You see, a person who has a vision, but doesn't have what it takes to bring that vision to pass will feel isolated. Understand that in places where poverty is the strongman, a person with a vision is rare. Most of the people in such areas have a lot of great ideas, but not many have an idea as to who they are or who they were created to be. Having a vision means having spiritual insight and being able to see yourself the way God created you. Nevertheless, the road to get to the you that you were designed to be seems long and almost impossible to navigate. Every time a procrastinator gets excited about a vision or an idea they've had, their excitement is short-lived and followed by an emotional crash. It's similar to having a caffeine crash. It starts off as a high energy moment, but ends in slothfulness and weariness, and this causes the procrastinator to go deeper into depression. That's why many people stop dreaming. They hate navigating the highs and lows associated with having a vision, especially when that vision seems to viciously taunt them. At the same time, the threat of being swallowed up by their own vision often feels more tangible and more credible than the reality that they're facing. For the procrastinator, it is easier to simply stop envisioning a future outside of their present realities than it is to keep dreaming dreams they feel can never become their realities. Because of this, the average procrastinator begins to imagine a future that they feel is more attainable than the visions they once had. The visions don't go away, but the people who are bound by procrastination simply change their minds about what they are envisioning. They start labeling the prophetic insights into their future as nothing more than mere fantasies or delusions of grandeur and this helps them to stop dreaming. In other words, the enemy teaches a person bound by the spirit of procrastination to kill their own visions.

The difference between a procrastinator and a person who simply dreams is... a procrastinator has insight into their future, but a dreamer has tapped into his or her own creative ability. A dreamer's dreams are oftentimes an answer to every problem, void and question the dreamer is presently faced with. A procrastinator, on the other hand, is (in most cases) a person who's been granted prophetic insight into his or her own future. Of course, procrastinators dream too, and they will often try to merge their dreams with their visions, but they lack the drive needed to pursue the "me" that they see. This is because they are subject to many strongholds, including, generational thinking, lack of knowledge, slothfulness and feelings of inferiority.

Mammon is the principality behind the religious notion that men and women of God (especially leaders) should not be wealthy. Again, this is because Mammon is the principality associated with numbers. Of course, such thinking derives from a lack of knowledge, and wherever there is a lack of knowledge, you will always find the doctrine of confusion. People who believe that men and women in leadership roles should not be wealthy are people who are generally okay with the world being wealthy. In other words, they are confused. God said that the wealth of the wicked is laid up for the just (see Proverbs 13:22), but Satan has convinced many in the church that Proverbs 13:22 was nullified by Matthew 19:24, which reads: *"And again I say unto you, It is easier for a camel to go through the eye of a needle, than for a rich man to enter into the kingdom of God."* Satan encourages believers to memorize one passage in each chapter; that way, they reject knowledge, and therefore, end up leaning to their own understanding.

Jesus said that it is easier for a camel to go through the eye of a needle than it is for a rich man to enter heaven, *but* that was not the end of his statement. This statement confused the disciples because our natural understanding says that it is impossible for a camel to go through the eye of a needle. In Matthew 19:26, the Lord challenged His disciples by helping them to understand that what is impossible to us is possible with God. Matthew 19:26 reads: *"But Jesus beheld them, and said unto them, 'With men this is impossible; but with God all things are possible.*'"

What does this mean? Jesus was clearly saying that it is possible (with God) for a camel to go through the eye of a needle. At the same time, He was not saying that it was wicked to be rich. He was addressing the state of the man. You see, Christ Himself was not a poor man. He simply tapped into Heaven anytime He wanted to. He had no need for anything, and anytime He went into a land, God had already chosen who He would stay with in that land. Nevertheless, the rich young ruler who approached Him was a wealthy man. That was his state; that was his reality. His wealth was the authority that ruled over him. Christ wanted to bring him outside of that state so that he could embrace salvation, but in doing so, he would have to make JEHOVAH his God. To do so, because of the state he was in, he would have to sell everything he owned. Understand that the rich young ruler was under the government and law of the spirit of Mammon and it is impossible to serve two gods.

Matthew 6:24 (KJV): No man can serve two masters: for either he will hate the one, and love the other; or else he will hold to the one, and despise the other. Ye cannot serve God and mammon.

Being rich was not the rich young ruler's sin. His sin was that he served Mammon, and everything he had was given to him by the spirit of Mammon. Remember Joseph of Arimathaea. He was the man who went to Pilate and asked for the body of Jesus. He was a rich man, and the Bible refers to him as a disciple of Christ, albeit, a secret disciple up until the death of Jesus.

The rich young ruler had been tested, but not because Jesus didn't know the state he was in. Jesus tested the ruler to show him the state he was in, and the Bible goes on to tell us that he walked away grieved. The

Mammon principality teaches its followers to love, worship and pursue money. It teaches them to depend on money and to fear its power. To a person under the government of Mammon, money is the principle thing, whereas, to someone who is submitted to YAHWEH, wisdom is the principle thing.

Demons under the rule of the Mammon principality are spirits of lack, spirits of destruction, spirits of pride, spirits of procrastination, spirits of slothfulness, spirits of addiction, what is commonly known as the "hustler" spirit, spirits of rejection, spirits of theft, spirits of entitlement, spirits of murder, etc. Basically, anyone in subjection to Mammon will serve the mighty dollar more than they serve the Almighty God. It goes without saying that each individual under the Mammon principality will serve that devil in different ways. For one man, his service may be to gamble away every penny that he earns. For another man, his service may be to steal the wealth of others. In the military of the thieving spirit, there are poor thieves and there are rich thieves. A poor thief may break into someone's home, steal someone's car, sell drugs or steal someone's identity. A rich thief may pay his workers less than what he owes them, fire some of his employees before they reach retirement age, pay others to use his private jet to bring drugs into the United States... drugs that eventually find themselves in the hands of the poor drug dealer who is also in submission to Mammon. For one man, his service may be to overwork himself. For another man, his service may be to not work at all, but instead, depend on the government to supply all of his needs, rather than depend on YAHWEH.

Philippians 4:19 (KJV): But my God shall supply all your needs according to his riches in glory by Christ Jesus.

The goal of the Mammon principality is to pervert the order of God, rob the people of God of their godly inheritance through Christ Jesus and distribute the wealth of the kingdom to the wicked. You see, even a man who loves and fears God can become a wicked man because of his love for money. When a man loves money, he will fall into the snares of the Mammon principality, and therefore, end up under its authority. That's why Christ warned the church by telling us that we cannot serve two gods. However, people who are under the Mammon principality aren't always truthful with themselves. They will never admit to loving money, pursuing money and exalting money over God. Instead, they'll justify their love of money by pointing out the fact that Abraham, David and Job were all rich men, which, of course, is true. Nevertheless, neither Abraham, David nor Job pursued riches; that's the difference. They pursued God and the closer you get to God, the more access you'll have to the wealth of the kingdom of God. That's why Solomon's prayer for wisdom set him up to be a very wealthy man. Wisdom isn't just knowledge because knowledge comes in layers (carnal and spiritual); wisdom is the heart, thoughts and knowledge of God. By asking for wisdom, Solomon unknowingly was asking to have the heart of God. His prayer didn't go amiss because his motives were right. He wanted to righteously govern the people of God. Nevertheless, anytime you ask God for something and it has nothing to do with His people, His kingdom or His glory, that is a prayer amiss because it is a selfish prayer. Such prayers come from the territory of the Mammon principality.

James 4:3 (KJV): Ye ask, and receive not, because ye ask amiss, that ye may consume it upon your lusts.

To understand the Mammon principality

and how it operates in the realm of the spirit, you must first understand how people under it operate in the natural. It basically creates a pyramid whereas it governs its followers through those it has appointed to be seated at the top of the pyramid. With Mammon, it's all about the numbers. For example, 90% of this world's wealth is owned by 10% of the population. The top one percent own almost half of all the global assets. If you want to know where the power is, follow the trail of money. In America alone, our president has very limited power. A lot of this nation's power is in the hands of Congress, and even with the president and Congress alone, this nation is being run by a total of 536 people. That is 535 voting members of Congress and the president. Understand that congressmen and women have their campaigns funded by billionaires and millionaires who control the vast majority of them through the strings of their purses.

This means that the ruling authority isn't Congress, nor is it the President. The ruling authority is the men and women who own 90 percent of this world's wealth, be they American or foreign. Of course, the majority of the wealthiest people in the world are under the control and government of the Mammon principality. **Ephesians 6:12 (KJV):** For we wrestle not against flesh and blood, but against principalities, against powers, against the rulers of the darkness of this world, against spiritual wickedness in high places.

King David had Israel counted, and this is what got David in trouble with God. He wanted to trust in the numbers and not God. By having Israel counted, David had unknowingly submitted to the government of Mammon and he had to be judged for his idolatry. Additionally, everyone under David's rule (all of Israel) fell under that judgment because whoever your head is will determine where your head is. Additionally, because David played by the numbers, God's judgment dealt with numbers. This was undoubtedly to teach David to not trust in numbers.

1 Chronicles 21:1-13 (ESV): Then Satan stood against Israel and incited David to number Israel. So David said to Joab and the commanders of the army, "Go, number Israel, from Beersheba to Dan, and bring me a report, that I may know their number." But Joab said, "May the Lord add to his people a hundred times as many as they are! Are they not, my lord the king, all of them my lord's servants? Why then should my lord require this? Why should it be a cause of guilt for Israel?" But the king's word prevailed against Joab. So Joab departed and went throughout all Israel and came back to Jerusalem. And Joab gave the sum of the numbering of the people to David. In all Israel there were 1,100,000 men who drew the sword, and in

Judah 470,000 who drew the sword. But he did not include Levi and Benjamin in the numbering, for the king's command was abhorrent to Joab.

But God was displeased with this thing, and he struck Israel. And David said to God, "I have sinned greatly in that I have done this thing. But now, please take away the iniquity of your servant, for I have acted very foolishly." And the Lord spoke to Gad, David's seer, saying, "Go and say to David, 'Thus says the Lord, Three things I offer you; choose one of them, that I may do it to you.'" So Gad came to David and said to him, "Thus says the Lord, 'Choose what you will: either three years of famine, or three months of devastation by your foes while the sword of your enemies overtakes you, or else three days of the sword of the Lord, pestilence on the land, with the angel of the Lord destroying throughout all the territory of Israel.' Now decide what answer I shall return to him who sent me." Then David said to Gad, "I am in great distress. Let me fall into the hand of the Lord, for his mercy is very great, but do not let me fall into the hand of man."

In relation to poverty, the Mammon principality seeks to disarm anyone who serves God or is chosen by God by simply removing what it believes to be one of man's most influential weapons: wealth. How does it get the people of God to give up their wealth? Through fear, lack of knowledge, religiousness that opposes righteousness, pride, evil association, false doctrines and lack of faith. Additionally, Mammon employs an army of individuals who will rise up against the wealthy people who dare to call themselves Christians. The people Mammon uses to rise up against the wealthy are stationed in the church, wearing Christian labels. Many of them stand behind the pulpit, wear religious garments and call themselves members of the five-fold ministry. They spew their false doctrines to a crowd of hungry but misled souls who wrestle with the same devils their leaders wrestle with... including the spirit of jealousy. Just as Joseph of Arimathaea was a secret disciple of Christ, these leaders are secret disciples of Mammon. They rise up against wealthy leaders... people appointed by God to distribute wealth to the nations and help the people of God. They do this by questioning their integrity. They encourage others to despise such leaders, and therefore, despise wealth. *If you despise wealth, you love poverty.* By doing so, they teach their followers that they must remain poor or at the lower end of the middle class if they ever want to enter heaven. This disarms and robs the believer through a lack of knowledge, and the believer's wealth ends up in the hands of the wicked. Followers of this belief often misquote 1 Timothy 6:10. They claim that money is the root of all evil when that is not

what God said. He said it is the *love* of
money that is the root of all evil.

God fights this principality by raising up
soldiers who He hides for an appointed
time… soldiers who He knows He can trust.
He empowers them with wisdom,
knowledge, understanding and wealth, and
when they are released, the Mammon
principality rises up against them from
within the church. However, every church
that Christ visits through these soldiers will
be given an opportunity to embrace the
truth or continue on in their lies. Those
who embrace the truth eventually grow up
to share in the wealth of the kingdom,
whereas, those who continue loving their
lies more than the truth eventually find
themselves perishing from a lack of
knowledge. Many of them find themselves
in predicaments where they need the very
wealth that they despised, but that wealth
is not available to them because they

attempted to cut off the hands that were designed to deliver it to them. It is at the peak (or end) of their lives that they realize that the people they served in ministry with can't truly help them. Instead, the army that they served with plans their funerals before they're even dead. Ironically enough, many of them also realize that the people who polluted their thinking with the doctrines that they followed were not actually opposed to wealth. They were jealous souls who opposed other leaders having the wealth they felt they were entitled to. Many of these leaders feel entitled because of their religious labels. Some think that their overabundance of knowledge entitles them to wealth, while others feel entitled because they have a Saul complex. They have witnessed God blessing the Josephs of the world and their hearts have grown bitter with envy. They served God for the money and not because of who He is. After preaching for decades on end, they reasoned within their own hearts that they were not wealthy because it was not God's will for them (or any man) who is in the church to be wealthy. Nevertheless, the Lord proved them wrong. They watched from afar (and sometimes up close) as a man or woman of God was elevated and enriched by God in less than a decade. Somehow, they had reasoned within their hearts that the Lord operated through seniority and not integrity, but when they saw God blessing and using a person they felt was not deserving of the power and the material wealth, their entitlement flared up. They disguised their bitterness by using snippets of scriptures, and then, twisting the words God said to fit their own selfish agendas. They began to openly rebuke and speak against anyone and everyone who dared to step into the very promised lands they themselves had never entered. Many of these leaders have (or had) small congregations, while others have (or had) large followings. They weren't in submission to the living God, Himself. They were (or are) servants of Mammon! That's why they are leading the people of God astray. They can't figure out why God has not used them at the capacity which they felt they deserved to be used at, and because of this, they have gathered an army of people to fight against the Word of God. Of course, most of these people don't realize they are fighting God; they simply trust the leaders who they are in submission to. It was the sinful lusts of their own hearts or their own lack of knowledge that led them to such leaders.

Matthew 15:14 (KJV): Let them alone: they be blind leaders of the blind. And if the blind lead the blind, both shall fall into the ditch.

Proverbs 4:19 (NIV): But the way of the wicked is like deep darkness; they do not know what makes them stumble.

Amos 3:3 (KJV): Can two walk together,

except they be agreed?

Mammon's agenda is clear. It wants to destroy God's kingdom on earth. It wants to put the power in the hands of the people who are in submission to it. It wants to gather an army for itself to fight against the people of God. It wants to pervert the plans and purposes of God. It wants to discredit God. It was (and is) the principality that governed the Babylonian system and it works together with the Baal principality. The Baal principality is the devil behind the works of the flesh. It encourages lust, selfish ambition, adultery, self-mutilation (tattoos, plastic surgery), addiction, fornication and just about anything tied to the flesh. Even though the Baal principality is a wicked and persistent ruler of the kingdom of darkness, it is a principality that is in subjection to the Mammon principality, therefore, anytime you come across Baal, you are in

Mammon's territory. Understand that the kingdom of darkness has order and every devil in it is assigned a rank. Mammon happens to be the largest principality of them all.

1 Timothy 6:10 (KJV): For the love of money is the root of all evil: which while some coveted after, they have erred from the faith, and pierced themselves through with many sorrows.

The Strongman of Poverty

I used to think that poverty was a spirit, but I wasn't entirely correct. Poverty is brought on by a spirit, of course, but poverty itself is a stronghold. Better yet, poverty is a form of perversion; it is a twisted state of mind. The mind of the person who is bound by poverty is altered to think opposite of the way God created it to think. Perversion isn't always sexual. To be perverted means that your mind, thoughts and beliefs are operating contrary to the way God created them, and when a perverse act is committed, it is simply a manifestation of one's heart condition. Nevertheless, people aren't entirely wrong when they speak against the spirit of poverty, but that's not its name. The correct name for the spirit in operation is the spirit of perversion. That's why many leaders have trouble casting that demon out; they don't know its true name! It goes without saying that the spirit of perversion is oftentimes accompanied by several demonic spirits, bringing a person possessed or influenced by it under the influence of Legion. Legion is believed to be two thousand or more demonic spirits. This belief is supported by Mark 5:6 when Jesus cast the legion of devils out of the man in the tombs. The Bible tells us that the devils went out of the man and entered the swine nearby, which totaled two thousand pigs. Those swine ran into the lake and drowned.

The spirits in operation have established Mammon's government in the person affected (or infected) by them. Again, Mammon is the principality (principle demon or prince) that governs the demons responsible for poverty. Baal is responsible for the system, or better yet, the demonic government itself. Baal is like the demonic congress that puts a system in place and ensures that it is run properly. Some people think that the Devil does not have an organized government, but he does. His government is well put together because his government is designed to mirror God's government. Every principality has a region to cover and several devils and powers under its rule. Just like everything in the natural and the spiritual, there are several ranks, categories and roles assigned to devils, powers and principalities. This order is also put in place in the realm of the earth, where Mammon assigns certain responsibilities to the people under its rule. With Mammon, there are the people who are considered high-ranking officials and these are the people Mammon enriches. They are the ones who hold roles similar to that of kings, nobles and knights. They are the ones who sit in high places and make decisions that will affect the United States and countries around the world. They are the ones who fund wars, terrorists and drug lords. Then, there are the people who are low-ranking officials and these are the people who Mammon robs. Low-ranking officials, to Mammon, are the peasants, or better yet, the slaves. They are the vagabonds used to balance the high-ranking people at the top. Many of these individuals are at the bottom of the totem pole and they depend on the government to supply their needs. The military of this class is what we refer to as gangs. A gang's purpose is to draw territorial lines and to ensure that the people of God do not unite. They are murderers, thieves, drug dealers and rapists who instill fear in their communities. The reason for this is... when the spirit of fear comes upon people, they go further and further away from God in their attempts to protect themselves. Many young men in gang-ridden neighborhoods join gangs to protect themselves and their families from opposing gangs. The ones who don't join gangs are often intimidated or killed, especially if it becomes clear that they are trying to better themselves through education. Mammon tries to ensure that everyone stays in the rank or role it has assigned them to, and when an individual tries to break that rank, Mammon sends its warriors out to attack that individual. That's why we call people who try to stop others from advancing "crabs in a bucket." We say these things, not realizing that we are not identifying a personal trait of the individuals who are being used as hindrances. Instead, we are identifying the characteristics of a warrior spirit, whether that spirit manifests through physical intimidation or through rumors designed to destroy a person's name.

A person bound by the stronghold of poverty will oftentimes struggle with low self-esteem, procrastination, impatience, slothfulness, jealousy and/ or depression.

Their view of money has been distorted by the spirit of perversion. They see money as the answer to all of their problems. Because of this, they will have an ungodly relationship with money, and this relationship will encourage them to become self-centered and manipulative. They will look for ways to advance themselves, even if that means that they have to inconvenience others to get what they want. They are the ones who will go into restaurants, overwork their waitresses, and then, call the manager after they've finished eating. They will accuse their waitresses of being inattentive, rude or prejudiced. This is an attempt from them to not have to pay for their food, or at least, get a huge discount. They don't consider that they may put the waitress's job at risk. They don't care whether the waitress has a family that she's struggling to feed or a sick parent that she's trying to take care of. They are selfishly motivated and their attempts to get a free meal have cost many people their jobs. They are also the ones who, when promoted at work, use whatever power entrusted to them to intimidate or terminate others who are not like them. They promote individuals who they can relate to, but anytime a man or woman of God is under their supervision, they will seek to demean, intimidate, slander or terminate that individual. Anytime they come across individuals with visions, whether those individuals are godly or ungodly, they will seek to demote them or make the workplace an uncomfortable place for them. This, of course, is to send a message to anyone and everyone who dares to dream. It is their attempt to rid the workplace of anyone they themselves cannot relate to or anyone they feel has the potential to replace them. Their mindsets keep them from advancing and Satan uses them to keep others from advancing.

There is order in every kingdom, including the kingdom of darkness, and the enemy uses the Mammon principality to set that order in the earth. God taught us to pray, "Thy will be done on earth as it is in heaven." However, Satan tries to mimic everything God does, so he tries to have everything that happens on earth line up to the order, or better yet, disorder of his kingdom. Someone bound by the strongman of poverty will want and love money, but he or she won't have the desire to sow the necessary seeds to get more money. This means, they aren't willing to work for it, and the ones who do work will overwork themselves. They will look for cunning ways to enrich themselves, even stooping so low that they'll masquerade themselves as men and women of God in their attempts to rob the church. Church leaders under the rule of this principality will oftentimes depend solely on their congregation to meet their needs, and anyone who is not considered a faithful sower will be diminished in their eyes. They will celebrate, promote and publicly recognize any and everyone who is a faithful sower or individuals who sow large amounts of money into their ministries, but they will not recognize or acknowledge the widow, for example, who sows today's equivalent of a mite. They will not acknowledge the college student who has little to nothing to give but simply needs godly instruction. They will not acknowledge the struggling alcoholic who is sincerely trying to turn his life around, unless, of course, their efforts will gain some sort of media attention. Many of these individuals will even speak curses (or attempt to speak curses) over the sheep they feel aren't great contributors to their ministries. On the other hand, they will speak blessings over wicked people if those people were to sow faithfully into them. **Isaiah 5:20 (ESV):** Woe to those who call evil good and good evil, who put darkness for light and light for darkness, who put bitter for sweet and sweet for bitter!

1 Timothy 6:3-10 (ESV): If anyone teaches a different doctrine and does not agree with the sound words of our Lord Jesus Christ and the teaching that accords with godliness, he is puffed up with conceit and understands nothing. He has an unhealthy craving for controversy and for quarrels about words, which produce envy, dissension, slander, evil suspicions, and constant friction among people who are depraved in mind and deprived of the truth, imagining that godliness is a means of gain. But godliness with contentment is great gain, for we brought nothing into the world, and we cannot take anything out of the world. But if we have food and clothing, with these we will be content. But those who desire to be rich fall into temptation, into a snare, into many senseless and harmful desires that plunge people into ruin and destruction. For the love of money is a root of all kinds of evils. It is through this craving that some have wandered away from the faith and pierced themselves with many pangs.

These leaders will seek to grow <u>their</u> own ministries, rather than allow God to grow <u>His</u> ministry in and through them. Because of this, their churches begin to take on the same order that the world is submitted under. It begins to take on the appearance of the Babylonian system, whereas, wealthy or well-to-do individuals will rank higher and have more say in the church than someone who is not a faithful giver, regardless of their spiritual condition. The "premium members" will have special seating at the front of the church, but those who need and want healing, deliverance and a genuine Word from God will be overlooked and treated as if they have entered some type of free clinic. When this happens, the church in question will become more and more perverse, loaning their microphones to politicians, celebrities and anyone who funds the church or brings public attention to it. They become hirelings of Baal, prostituting their gifts and their anointing for money, power and recognition. Those who follow them will repeatedly find themselves struggling with sin and wrestling with the Lord when He tries to warn them about their leaders. They will attempt to rebuke the voice of the living God in favor of continuing their now ungodly relationships with their leaders. It won't be long before they fall into the very ditch or sin that their blind leaders have led them into. This is why it is very important to seek God about the church or the people you give the charge of watching over your soul. Only God knows who has the love, wisdom and the spiritual capacity to cover you. Any other leader will uncover you in their attempts to grow their ministries.

Before long, they will become greedy, self-seeking, false prophets who prophesy good over any and everyone who sows into their ministries. Should those people choose to leave their ministries, they will attempt to speak curses over them and/or withdraw the good prophecies they once spoke over them. The reality is... this does happen in many of today's churches!

The stronghold of poverty not only teaches its captives to become complacent in their lack, it also teaches them to love money, even though wealth seems to be almost impossible for them to obtain. The Mammon spirit is the reason for this. It teaches its followers that they can cross over the barriers that separate the impoverished from the prosperous, but to do this, they must be willing to take drastic measures. It's similar to a gang initiation, where gang members have to undergo a few tests to prove their loyalty (and their desperation). Additionally, to ascend the ranks of a gang, members must be willing to commit heinous crimes. They must be willing to risk everything, including their lives, for this promotion. Those who aren't willing to step outside of their sinful comfort zones spend their lives working, gambling and hoping for a change to come. Those who are willing to up the ante and spend a large portion of their lives being used by the Mammon principality to hurt, rob and instill fear in people are oftentimes enriched by this wicked principality. As the adage says, "Hurt people hurt people," meaning that the very people they hurt will oftentimes seek solace in sin, and eventually, go out and start hurting others as well. It's similar to a virus, whereas, anyone who comes in contact with a hurt person is eventually hurt by that person. They then become the very vessels Satan uses to hurt people, and the cycle continues.

Remember, a stronghold is a place where people feel safe. Understand that the stronghold of poverty is a place where impoverished people actually feel safe. That's because they are surrounded by people who are like themselves, and the reality is... people who know you personally and can identify with you will oftentimes defend you, watch over your home and risk their lives for you. The stronghold of poverty is a place and mindset that serves as a comfort zone for billions of people.

When I was growing up in poverty, I didn't know that my family was poor. I knew that some people had more money than us; that was all. Nevertheless, I felt comfortable in my reality, mindset, neighborhood and amongst my peers. I didn't worry about getting robbed, raped or killed. My greatest fear was standing out too much.

People who are bound by the stronghold of

poverty are often surrounded by lots of people. They have many friends, or at least, people they think are their friends. They are very sociable, and many are very, very kind because everyone around them is struggling with something. Most people learn to relate to one another in poverty and most people learn to empathize with others. Nevertheless, as kind as some people can be, there are others who won't be so kind to impoverished souls whose futures appear to be bright. That's why it is very dangerous for a young man growing up in an impoverished area to be ambitious, or to let others know that he is ambitious. The Mammon principality would seek to have him "humbled" because he's seeking to advance himself, rather than doing what it takes for Mammon to advance him. In other words, he would serve as a light to many people whose realities were similar to his... people who had come to believe that they couldn't be anything more than what they already are. He would be a threat to Mammon's government, and for this reason, he would find himself being harassed, attacked and possibly even killed by the guys from his neighborhood who accepted defeat as their realities. Again, these guys are unknowingly soldiers for Mammon, assigned to ensure that no one dares to go outside of the ghettos, trailer parks and slums that Mammon has locked them into. The same goes for women. Any woman who has a vision will not sound, behave or think like her peers and this would make her a target for their ridicule, attacks and fear tactics. To justify their "war" against her, many of her peers would label her as "thinking she's better than them" and they would seek to humble or humiliate her. If she's attractive, many would seek to scar her and hopefully remove what they believe to be her ticket out of poverty. Their goal would be to make her fit in with them or submit to their rule. She would have to learn to be a person who doesn't draw attention to herself. She would have to become a person who fears them and does whatsoever they say. In other words, she would become imprisoned by the spirit of fear, and if she refused to submit to their authority, they would escalate their attacks against her. This is the reality for many people, but they don't have voices to share with the world why they are too afraid to speak out against crime and why they are too afraid to dream. They are in strongholds, and while they may fear for their lives, they still feel safe enough to remain quiet and try not to draw attention to themselves. At the same time, many men and women who live in impoverished areas aren't afraid to be themselves. They endure the attacks, the ridicule, and the fear tactics, and many of them rise up to be some of the greatest success stories around because they refused to be intimidated.

Proverbs 14:20 (ESV): The poor is disliked even by his neighbor, but the rich has many friends.

Proverbs 19:7 (ESV): All a poor man's brothers hate him; how much more do his friends go far from him! He pursues them with words, but does not have them.

People who've endured poverty and everything that comes with it often have experiences that not only sharpen them, but they have stories that encourage others. Some of America's most intelligent people are somewhere hidden in the slums with no voice and no identity. Many of these souls perish, never having the opportunity to share their gifting with the world. This undoubtedly was Satan's plan all along. He wants to ensure that God's people never rise up to their God-given potential. He wants to ensure that anyone he's oppressed never sees the light of success, especially if that person is saved, sanctified and filled with the Holy Spirit. This would give too much glory to God and teach others that they don't have to go into sin to find success. After all, that's the lesson Mammon teaches to the people in which it oppresses. It teaches them that they have to go to drastic measures to come out of their realities. Those who are hungry enough or desperate enough will go to great (wicked) lengths to get the money and recognition they feel they are entitled to. On the other side of the spectrum, a rich man (or woman) is encouraged to go to great lengths to keep their money and to grow it. Greed is oftentimes a rich man's prison. For those in poverty, the rich man with all of the money appears to have it all. That's because the general mindset of people who have little to no money is that money is the answer to all of their problems. Nevertheless, a rich man's reality is oftentimes not what it appears to be. He's surrounded by people he cannot trust and it is hard for him to find genuine love, so he's encouraged to marry women whose families are successful like himself. If he grew up rich, he has trouble relating to the rest of the world. He's often encouraged by his family to portray a reality that he does not have. He's encouraged to be on his best behavior while in public because in many well-to-do homes, the family's greatest fear (besides losing their money) is public scrutiny. They are bound by the opinions of others, especially if they want to continue growing or maintaining their wealth. To give their children some "reality checks" designed to help them build their character, many wealthy people send their children to boarding schools.

One of the spirits that bind people in poverty is the spirit of fear. The average person who lives in poverty or just above the poverty line fears success. Sure, they want money and they want to have better lives, but they fear what comes with money and power. After all, most people have seen someone get swallowed whole by their love of money or lose their lives trying to pursue it. Even though it is not discussed, most people in and outside of poverty understand that they will have to change mentally to reach their successful places. Nevertheless, there are doors that are open that would allow them to avoid God's process of change and go straight into their wealthy places. These doors include, but are not limited to: gambling, Hollywood (music and/or television), selling or transporting drugs, stealing from the wealthy or the government, blackmail, etc. Those who want to gather their success, choose legal ways to get it, but it goes without saying that Satan requires that anyone who enters Hollywood through music or media (when they come through him) must be willing to lead the viewers astray. He doesn't mind them calling themselves Christians as long as they represent him in their works, lives and music. He doesn't mind them calling themselves Christians and singing about God as long as their lives don't line up with God's Word. He encourages secular people to sing gospel music because he knows the world is watching them. These souls will sing the gospel, but everything about them will represent the secular realm. This brings about confusion and complacency. Many in the church are confused when they see such artists, and for others, they feel justified in their sins and their lifestyles after following these artists. People who feel justified in their sins will convince themselves that any other artist who practices holiness is simply faking their walks. Because of this, they will monitor the lives of any artist who God has risen up, and like Satan himself, they will look for sin in that artist. They will sift through the artist's music and monitor the artist's life, all the while, disguising themselves as loyal followers. Nevertheless, should the artist make a mistake or backslide, they will be the first to point out the artist's mishap. When one of their own falls, on the other hand, they will be the first to say, "Let him who is without sin cast the first stone," or "Nobody's perfect." The world loves and will support its own, but will always rise up against the remnant of God.

John 15:19 (ESV): If you were of the world, the world would love you as its own; but because you are not of the world, but I chose you out of the world, therefore the world hates you.

How can someone fear success, but love money? It's simple. Success is all-inclusive, whereas, it consists of peace, joy, perfect health and prosperity. Of course, prosperity varies in definition with each individual person. The love of money consists of lusts

and selfish ambitions. A person who loves
money will envision a better life for him or
herself and he or she will believe that
wealth will bring them peace and joy. After
all, such an individual believes that the
solution to every problem they have is
money. Because of this, money has
become their god, which places them in
submission to the Mammon principality
and a citizen of Baal's system. Of course,
the Bible tells us in Ecclesiastes 10:19 that
money answers all things, or better yet,
money is the answer to everything.
Nevertheless, money answers natural
things, but cannot answer spiritual things.
This means that a person who pursues and
acquires wealth outside of God may be able
to solve many of their natural problems
with money, but their spiritual problems
would be without remedy. They wouldn't
be able to buy love, joy, peace, faith,
longsuffering, gentleness, goodness,
meekness or temperance for themselves

since all are fruit of the Holy Spirit. For this reason, many people who acquire wealth outside of God find themselves overburdened, depressed, fearful and unable to enjoy the very peace we sometimes take for granted. When God enriches His people, however, He first endows them with the fruit of the Holy Spirit, for this, in itself, is spiritual wealth. It is the wealth that keeps us, polishes our character and gives us the wisdom, knowledge and understanding we'll need to live long, purpose-filled lives.

Proverbs 10:22 (ESV): The blessing of the LORD makes rich, and he adds no sorrow with it.

The strongman of poverty is nothing more than a mindset that's held together by a lack of knowledge, stabilized by complacency and guarded by demonic spirits. One guarding spirit you will always confront when dealing with the strongman of poverty is the spirit of pride. This devil encourages the person bound to puff up against the truth. It encourages them to defend themselves because it makes them think that anyone who speaks the truth is rising up against them. The spirit of pride is always accompanied by the spirit of offense, which is also a guarding spirit. The spirit of offense is the reactive spirit that triggers the flesh to respond. Poverty's stronghold on the human mind serves as a wall, ensuring that wisdom, knowledge and understanding do not enter any of its captives hearts. Instead, poverty's captives will want to pour out their understandings and the contents of their own hearts, rather than receive sound doctrine. This is what ensures that they stay bound and they remain citizens of the demonic government run by Mammon.

Proverbs 1:7 (ESV): The fear of the LORD is the beginning of knowledge; fools despise wisdom and instruction.

Proverbs 18:2 (ESV): A fool takes no pleasure in understanding, but only in expressing his opinion.

Symptoms of Poverty

Poverty isn't just a stronghold of the mind;
spiritually speaking, it is a disease of the
soul. Our souls, of course, are comprised of
our mind, will and emotions. This means
that poverty affects our thinking, and
therefore, controls what manifests as our
realities.

Most people think poverty is an economic
condition, and this misguided thinking
helps them to either remain in poverty, use
the wrong tools to come out of poverty or
continue judging people who are
impoverished. The truth of the matter is
that people in poverty aren't there because
their finances are severely limited. Many
are there because they lack the necessary
knowledge to operate above where they
are. In some cases, the individuals don't

lack the knowledge, but they are too fearful to apply that knowledge to their lives. Again, one strength that the devil has over many people in and outside of poverty is the fear of other people and their opinions. This weapon has been the most effective weapon to keep people from elevating or accelerating outside of ensuring that they don't crave or pursue knowledge.

Most of the people who have the necessary knowledge lack understanding and this too can be crippling. For example, many people who are impoverished know that poverty is not God's will for them and they know what the Bible says about poverty, but they don't understand why they are in poverty and how to get out of it. The spirits of procrastination, fear and slothfulness comes forward to ensure that they never seek to gain that understanding. For this reason, many people in (and outside) of poverty read very few books, especially books about economics. They may find themselves attracted to fictional books and romance novels, but the desire to read or view anything that could be beneficial to their lives is simply not there. If you don't believe this, take a friend who is bound by the strongman of poverty and play a movie that's entertaining to him, and you'll notice how engaged he is with that movie. He may laugh, talk and become very animated while watching the movie. On a different day, play something that teaches about saving money, cleaning up one's credit or self-advancement and you'll notice how slothful he becomes. He'll either fall asleep, excuse himself to the bathroom frequently or leave. That's because the spirits behind poverty will treat his emotions like a light switch. When he's watching or reading something that doesn't help him, they will allow him to stay engaged, or better yet, turned on, but when he is watching or reading anything that would help him to overcome them, they'll simply flip a switch in his emotions. After all, strongholds occur in the soulish realm and they affect our mind, will and emotions.

Since poverty is a disease, that means, it has to fall under one of two labels: curable or incurable. With God, everything is curable. This means that anyone who wants to come outside of poverty can do so, but of course, this is made harder in certain countries, albeit, never impossible. Below are ten of poverty's nastiest symptoms.

1. **Lack of Wisdom, Knowledge and Understanding-** This is diagnosed when a person opens his or her mouth and by the choices that he or she makes. Lack of wisdom, knowledge and understanding is a direct result of one not reading his or her Bible or not seeking God for understanding. You see, we can read

the Bible in our carnal minds and attempt to understand what we've read, but by doing so, we end up doing the very thing the Bible tells us not to do and that is to lean on our own understanding. When we lean to our own understanding, we try to take new information and run it through our belief systems and what we currently understand or think we understand. This is how most false religions are started. Someone takes the Bible, does not pray about what they are reading and attempts to understand it with the knowledge they've obtained through others or over the courses of their lives. They don't seek the Lord about what they're reading, and therefore, they end up full of false information and under the doctrine of confusion.

2. **Overwhelming Desire to Spend-** People bound by the strongman of

poverty cannot rest unless they have spent almost every dime in their accounts or they've spent most of their money. Most people bound by poverty are used to having a certain amount of money each week or month. That specific number represents their comfort zone. (Remember, Mammon is all about the numbers.) Anytime they receive a lump sum of money (income tax refunds, school checks, child support, etc.), their minds are flooded with thoughts of what they want and need. They cannot rest until they've spent the money back down to what they're accustomed to having. Because of this, an individual bound by poverty's strongman will go on a spending spree anytime he or she has an overabundance of money. Additionally, the individual will spend money on things that he or she does not need, rarely taking the time out to put money away for what we refer to as a "rainy day." The presence of more money than they are accustomed to takes their peace away, and even though they aren't sad or depressed, they still don't have peace. Instead, they become overly excited and overly anxious to spend their abundance.

3. **Overwhelming Desire to Fit in-** People who are not bound by the strongman of poverty don't often consider (or care) what others think about them. Instead, they've learned to expect ridicule, persecution and the like. Nevertheless, people bound by the strongman of poverty do care about what others say and/or think about them, even though many will declare the opposite. People who are bound by this stronghold tend to follow the trends and fads set by

Hollywood or set by some of their peers.

I remember growing up in a lot of impoverished neighborhoods (we moved almost every year up until I was twelve or thirteen). In each of these neighborhoods, there was a young girl who'd gained the respect of her peers through fighting. She would always loudly proclaim that she did not care what others thought and she appeared to be a leader, but it simply took getting to know her to see and understand the truth about her. She cared what others thought and that's why she'd learned to fight so well. She didn't want to be the object of ridicule, and in many cases, she didn't have the beauty or the money that some of the neighborhood's most popular girls had. In many cases, she didn't have the loving parents that others had, so she learned to defend herself, and when she realized that she was a great fighter, she made a name for herself by fighting any and everyone who'd either offended her, challenged her, or posed a threat to her reputation. She didn't fit in, so she found a way to gain respect; that way, she could stand out on her own terms.

4. **Overwhelming Desire to Appear Wealthy-** You'll notice that in most impoverished neighborhoods, there are people driving luxury vehicles, wearing name brand clothes and adorning themselves with expensive jewelry. That's because captives of poverty don't have the money they need to gain the respect of others, so they gain their respect through illusion. They pretend to have more than most of the people in their neighborhoods because they want

the respect and adoration of man.
Additionally, some of Mammon's
soldiers stationed in Hollywood
(rappers, hip hop artists, pop stars,
etc.) have illegally obtained their
wealth. In other words, they didn't
get their wealth or notoriety from
God. They were elevated by the
enemy with the assignment to keep
others from rising. Because of this,
there are many celebrities who dress,
think and speak in a way that people
in poverty can relate to. In a sense,
they become representatives or
ambassadors for the people who can
relate most to them. They serve as
symbols to their followers that there
is another way to success outside of
changing their minds. Their followers
see them as spokesmen who can
help those who don't share in their
realities better understand them,
their languages and their cultures. Of

course, this stops the culture in which the celebrity represents from being contained to a certain area, and people searching for their own identities may then began to submit to this culture. Of course, by doing so, they apply for citizenship under the Mammon rule.

5. **Addiction to Debt-** When I was the strongman's captive, I could not stop putting myself in debt. I was always getting loans, cash advances or applying for credit cards. I worked hard for the money I had, but I didn't earn enough money to live the lavish lifestyle I desired, so I looked for ways to satisfy my cravings for more money. Every time I got approved for a loan or I received a credit card, I would get overly excited. I knew that the next few days would be full of smiles for me and I couldn't wait to go shopping.

People who are in subjection to poverty are always putting themselves in debt. They don't do this because they think they can repay the debt. Oftentimes, people are addicted to the highs and lows associated with having money to spend. Spending money is easy (and fun), but paying that money back is a horror story in itself.

6. **Spending Money Owed-** Sure, you've got bills to pay, but there's a lot of fun to be had, and if you pay those bills back when they say you have to pay them back, you may end up missing out on a lot of fun. This is truly the mentality of individuals bound by the strongman of poverty. Let's say that a famous celebrity will be in town on the fifth of next month, and that happens to be the day that you are supposed to pay off a cash loan that you have. A few of your

friends call you and ask if you're going to the concert, which is now shaping up to be the event of the year. Like most people in poverty, you begin to measure your situation against the situation of the creditor. He's better off than you are. He's a millionaire. Surely, he can wait a little longer for his money. You then review your wages and determine that you can shift a few bills around. You happily agree to go to the concert and you call the creditor to let him know that you will be late paying him the money you owe. Of course, the creditor isn't too happy about your delinquency, so the company adds late fees to your payment. Now, you're not so happy because this places you further in debt than you wanted to be. You blame the creditor for your situation, when in truth, you are to blame. You had the money to pay the creditor back, but you chose to pay that money to a celebrity so that he or she could entertain you.

People under the rule of poverty are almost always spending the money that they owe to others. Of course, this mentality is a symptom of the stronghold against their minds. You see, when you don't pay back the money you owe to others, you become a slave to the people you owe money to.

Romans 13:7-8 (ESV): Pay to all what is owed to them: taxes to whom taxes are owed, revenue to whom revenue is owed, respect to whom respect is owed, honor to whom honor is owed. Owe no one anything, except to love each other, for the one who loves another has fulfilled the law.

7. **Borrowing Money and Becoming**

Angry When the Time Comes to Pay it Back- So, you've borrowed money from someone or some company, and the time has come to pay that money back. You don't want to pay it back because you have other bills or other things that you want to do with that money, so you begin to review the financial status of the person or company you borrowed the money from. Let's say that you've borrowed money from your older sister who happens to be more financially stable than you are. The time has come to pay her the money back, but you hope that she doesn't make you repay her or she gives you more time to repay her. Because of this thinking, you intentionally do not call her or answer any of her calls. Finally, you listen to a voicemail that she left for you and on the voicemail she's asking about her money. You've already spent the money or made plans with it, so you find yourself angry with your sister because you think that she's being insensitive towards your "situation." After all, she has the money she needs to pay her bills, so why is she pestering you? Believe it or not, this is the attitude of a person bound by the strongman of poverty. When I was a child, I watched helplessly as people borrowed money from my mother. I saw how well they treated her when she agreed to loan them the money, but when the time came for them to pay it back, I saw how aggressive and condescending they were towards her.

The same goes with paying off bills owed to companies. The kindest people to walk into a loan company are the ones who want to borrow money, but the meanest people to walk into a loan company are the ones who owe money to that company. The general attitude of a person in debt is to take offense with the creditor for making them pay the money back or not allowing them to pay the money back at a pace they feel would be more beneficial to them.

8. **Demeaning Thoughts Towards Wealthy Individuals and People Outside of Your Own Mindset-** The truth is that we cannot relate to anyone who is outside of our realities or outside of a reality we once were a part of. Because of this, we, as a people, have trouble supporting anyone we cannot understand. A rich man who cannot relate to us may come off as insensitive and ignorant, and while this may be true about him, we are also ignorant of his

reality. Nevertheless, because most of us who grew up in poverty were taught that a rich man's reality was better than our own, we learned to see people who were born wealthy as foolish souls with too much money in their hands and too much time on their hands. This caused many of us to become just as ignorant of the rich man's reality as he was about ours. Because of this, many people born and raised in poverty will support celebrities and millionaires who have mindsets or testimonies similar to their own, but cannot and will not support individuals whose testimonies are that they grew up rich. Of course, they are different. Nevertheless, they are as different to us as a foreigner is to us. People who never take the time out to get to know others outside of the people they feel they can relate to are oftentimes insensitive towards others, be they poor or rich. It goes without saying, however, that if we were to open our hearts and our minds to people who are different than ourselves, we may be able to overcome the strongman of poverty by simply allowing new knowledge into our lives. For example, I was married to an African man and his culture was completely different than our culture. Before I met him, I was very ignorant of his reality as well as the reality of many people in Africa. Initially, every ounce of knowledge or information I received either came from the television or from someone else's experiences. When I met my ex, I asked him many ignorant questions and I found that many of the questions or misconceptions I had were put to rest. I learned to be more sensitive towards others because I'd met many people from various countries all over Africa as well as other continents. I also learned to understand that a wealthy man's reality was no better than my own. He simply had a different set of problems than I had, but he hurts the same way, bleeds the same way and dies the same way as every one of us.

9. **Money Becomes Your Drug of Choice-** An ex of mine pointed something out about a few of my family members. My family, of course, was (and still are) bound by the strongman of poverty, and therefore, leaned to the United States government for their needs. One of my family members received a monthly check, and every time he received his check, his confidence would peek. He walked in a slouched position and his countenance was down when he had no money, but

when he got his check, he held his
head high, his shoulders went back
and he smiled at everyone. It wasn't
long, however, before he'd spent
most, if not all, of his money and he'd
return to his slouched position and
not-so-chipper attitude. Another
family member of mine did the same
thing, but she did not receive a
monthly check from the government.
She actually worked for her money,
but anytime she got paid, she'd
become joyful, positive and
reassured. When I was bound by this
strongman, I was the same way. My
confidence levels were at their
highest when I had money in my
pockets, even when that money was
supposed to go towards bills.
Nevertheless, when the money was
gone, I wasn't the most chipper
human being to be around. I lived
for payday.

What does this mean? People who are bound by poverty feel high when they have money, but when the money is gone, they sober up to their realities. With God, however, people are joyful regardless of what they have in their accounts.

10. **Living by Chance and Not by Faith-** An impoverished man with no faith will trust in his own devices to feed his family. Because of this, he will sow the seeds from the labor of his hands into casinos, lottery tickets and get-rich-quick schemes. These get-rich-quick schemes promise him a better life without the process we must all endure to enter our wealthy places. The process towards wealth through gambling or any other godless device seems to be less tedious and less demanding than the process required by God. Casinos depend on his seeds. Lottery

companies depend on his seeds. With every seed sown, he places himself further into debt, which means, he's repeatedly renewing his contract as a slave to the people he owes. Nevertheless, he's able to maintain a fraction of his sanity through his faith in the slot machines, lottery tickets and whatever opportunities he believes that chance will hand him. Many of these individuals pray to God and ask Him to violate His own seed time and harvest law and bless them with an overabundance of cash through their gambling. It goes without saying, however, that this is a prayer amiss. God will not violate His own laws, so when someone wins, for example, the lottery, the win did not come from God. It came from the enemy, and as such, the money is accursed.

The Truth About Debt

From the moment I entered this earth, my dad began to introduce me to poverty. Of course, he told me about God, took me to church and read the Bible to me, but he demonstrated poverty to me. So, poverty was what I knew. I learned to be religious... saying things I knew God wanted to hear, but my works were ungodly.

I can remember being eight years old, sitting at the kitchen table with my dad. During that time, advertisers would send out multiple advertisements in a bundle. These ads were postcard shaped forms that advertised books, toys and other products. They would be wrapped in a clear package and we'd sort through them to see which ones read, *"No postage if mailed in the USA."* When we found the ones that did not require postage, we'd separate them from the rest and we'd start filling them out. My dad would drop the forms into the mailbox and we'd anxiously await what I saw as free stuff. I knew that the companies required payments for the stuff they were shipping to us; after all, the bills would follow the stuff, but my dad would toss those bills into the trash. Because of this, I saw debt as a cat and mouse game between the lender and the borrower. I didn't think I was hurting anyone; after all, I was eight years old and my dad was teaching me to get free stuff. I saw them as huge companies who weren't affected by my dad's choice to order a few things from them and not pay them. When the bills came, I didn't worry about giving them to my dad. I knew he'd tell me to toss them in the trash, so I took the initiative to throw away anything that remotely resembled a bill. Little did I know that this mindset was the catalyst behind the strongman of poverty and it would weigh me down for years to come.

A few weeks before I turned eighteen, I started getting a lot of credit card applications. I'd even received a few cards that I hadn't signed up for. I simply needed to activate them. I ordered every credit card that was offered to me and I went on one shopping spree after another. Nevertheless, I tried to fashion myself as a responsible woman, so I made attempts to pay off my debt by paying the minimum fee each month. When I realized that the minimum fee was not bringing down the amount I owed to each company, I lost my zeal for paying off the cards. I felt like the companies were robbing me, so I began to see my creditors the way my dad taught me to see them. I saw them as rich people who'd rob the poor to fatten their own pockets (if allowed), so I became my very own Robin Hood. I took from the rich creditors and gave to my poor self. I returned to the ways that I had been taught.

By the time I was 24 years of age, my credit score was around four to five hundred and I was married to a man whose credit score was just as bad as mine, if not worse. We would go to furniture companies looking to buy furniture on credit, and of course, we knew we had to pay them back. While waiting to see if we qualified, we would hear the printers printing off what sounded like hundreds of pages of documents and we'd often joke about whose credit report was being printed at that moment. Additionally, during our marriage, we had two or three cars repossessed and our stack of unpaid bills continued to mount. We both dealt with our debt in different ways. I found denial to be the easiest way for me to cope with the depression that came with the mounting debt, but he wanted to write all of the bills down and stress over them.

We would often argue because he'd write down what needed to be paid, and then, he wanted to go over his list with me. I knew that we wouldn't come to any resolve outside of him saying something that would stress me all the more, so I refused to look at any of the lists he'd created. As if unpaid credit cards weren't enough, our utilities would often be disconnected for non-payment. We'd then attempt to have them reconnected in a different name. When this didn't work, we'd just sit in our home without lights or heat. For the most part, we would pay our electric bill (I think it was probably disconnected once or twice), but our gas was almost always disconnected. I remember us boiling water to add to our bath water, and we purchased a couple of kerosene heaters to keep our home warm during the winter. To make matters worse, we were almost always entangled in cash advances. We'd have two cash advances out at a time, and every time we got paid, we would pay off one advance and write another one. We were really bad off, even though we lived in a huge home, drove nice cars and had our home furnished like the home of a millionaire. I didn't realize the importance of paying bills until we tried to buy a house. We were denied time and time again until we came across an agency that loaned money to high-risk applicants. It goes without saying that we lost that house to foreclosure after we started going through a divorce. We even filed bankruptcy but didn't follow through with it because we were required to pay off some unpaid taxes. Unpaid bills were our kryptonite. Amazingly enough, I was a Christian then, even though I was a babe in Christ.

After we started going through a divorce, I met the man who would become my second husband. He was from Africa, but he was finishing up his schooling in

Germany. Before I met Roger, I was like most Americans. I thought of Africans as poor people who'd easily jump at the opportunity to get free stuff, but I was wrong. Roger was not bound by poverty's strongman, and after we were married, I tried to bind him with it unknowingly, but he wouldn't budge. We'd just moved to Florida and we needed furniture for our new apartment. Roger had just started a new job and he'd made it pretty clear that we'd likely go months on end without any furniture. All we had was an air mattress and I wasn't used to sleeping in an empty place. Up until that point, I didn't mind going into debt to get what I wanted, but Roger minded. He was passionately against debt and he'd often tell me that if we couldn't afford to buy it with cash, we weren't going to have it. I was furious. I told myself that Roger was used to not having anything, so he was about to have me driving around in a lemon and sleeping on an air mattress for the rest of our lives. This infuriated me all the more and I became more determined to convince him that credit wasn't a bad thing. Nevertheless, Roger would not budge. A couple of months after moving to Florida, we finally purchased a couch, and a month later, we purchased a bed. Roger's way was working. Our apartment began to fill up slowly, and before long, we had a car to call our own. I didn't go out and get a traditional job; instead, I started my own business while Roger worked. Roger didn't require that I pay any bills except the cell phone bill and buy groceries.

During our marriage, I began to adapt to a debt-free life. I loved the freedom of not worrying about unpaid bills. It wasn't long before I'd adopted Roger's reasoning and I refused to rent or lease anything. Roger's motto became my motto: If we couldn't afford to buy it with cash, we weren't going to get it. I stayed away from credit cards and any form of debt, and slowly, but surely, items began to fall off my credit report because the seven year window had passed. Once Roger and I divorced, I maintained my no-debt lifestyle, and when I checked my credit report, it was without blemish. My credit score had risen well above seven hundred. Of course, I praised God because I knew that He'd forgiven me for my sins... including my unpaid debt. The truth is I was no longer the woman who'd once created the debt because God had grown me up in Him and taught me Kingdom principles. That old poverty mindset had passed away because I'd broken past the stronghold of poverty to embrace new understanding.

It was two years after Roger and I broke up when I decided to get a credit card. The only reason I agreed to get the card was because a few people told me that I would need to get a card to rebuild my credit. I went into a retail store to purchase a coat one day, and when the cashier offered me a credit card, I went ahead and signed up for it. This opened the door for an attack that almost wiped out my finances. I didn't realize it then, but anytime you disobey God, the enemy will use that opportunity to attack you in the area that you disobeyed God in. What did God say about debt?

Romans 13:8 (ESV): Owe no one anything, except to love each other, for the one who loves another has fulfilled the law.

Proverbs 22:7 (ESV): The rich rules over the poor, and the borrower is the slave of the lender.

Deuteronomy 15:6 (ESV): For the LORD your God will bless you, as he promised you, and you shall lend to many nations, but you shall not borrow, and you shall rule over many nations, but they shall not rule over you.

Proverbs 22:26-27 (ESV): Be not one of

those who give pledges,
who put up security for debts. If you have
nothing with which to pay, why should your
bed be taken from under you?

After I charged my new coat to my card, my
finances went under a major attack. At first,
my check engine light started coming on
and my car starting jerking. I took it to a
mechanic shop and they said that my
throttle was sticking. I ended up paying
over three hundred dollars to have it fixed.
A month later, the gear shift in my car got
stuck and I had to call a mobile mechanic to
fix it. Thankfully, the issue was a blown fuse
and the mechanic charged me one hundred
dollars to repair it. The next day, my car
was blowing out white smoke, getting hot
and I saw water running to the ground. I
called the mobile mechanic back and he
told me that it sounded like a blown head
gasket. He told me that I needed to have
my car towed to a shop, so I found a shop

and had the car towed there. The mechanic
confirmed that the issue was a blown head
gasket, plus, he named other things that
were allegedly wrong with my car, including
a damaged water pump. I paid him over
fifteen hundred dollars to replace the
gasket and the water pump, but I decided
to hold off on the brakes and the oil pan he
said I needed. After all, I had never had a
problem with my brakes before, plus, my
car had been with a few mechanics and no
one ever said I had a leaking oil pan.
Nevertheless, after I got the car back from
the mechanic, I started hearing my brakes
scrub for the first time. I was angry with
the mechanic because I believed that he'd
done some damage to my car in an
attempt to extort more money out of me;
after all, I was a woman living alone. I
ended up taking my car to Pep Boys to
have my brakes replaced and my heart
broke when the mechanic there told me
that one of my car's calipers needed to be

replaced. I ended up paying close to five hundred dollars to have that car fixed. A few days after I had the calipers, rotaries and brakes replaced, my car started getting hot again. By this time, I was almost numb because I'd taken a huge hit financially. I knew I was under attack and I tried to figure out which direction the attack was coming from. I took the car back to the mechanic shop that had replaced my blown head gasket, and to my horror, the mechanic said that my car needed a new radiator. I was livid. He wanted me to pay him an additional three hundred dollars and I wasn't going to give him another dime of my money. I drove my car to another mechanic shop and the mechanics there subtly confirmed what I'd suspected. The other mechanic had been ripping me off. I paid them to replace my radiator, but after the radiator was in the car, it continued to get hot. My new mechanics said that the gasket on my car was dirty, which meant that either the other mechanic hadn't replaced it or he didn't have it pressurized. They believed that my gasket was blown or the head had split, so they encouraged me to go back to the other mechanic to see what he was willing to do. Frustrated, I called the first mechanic and told him what the other mechanics had reported to me. He had me to bring the car back in, and of course, he gave me a lecture about how reputable his company was. They fixed the car and he was all too happy to report back that the issue was simply a bad thermostat.

I went into prayer, looking for the door in which Satan was attacking my finances through. Was I sowing seeds in bad ground? I prayed and the Lord revealed three different directions in which the enemy was attacking me, but I'd opened the door for him the moment I'd placed my first (and only) charge to my new credit card. It goes without saying that I rushed to pay off my card's balance and vowed to cut it up and never use it again. The devil waited a long time for me to open a door for him to attack me financially, and when I finally opened that door, he came in and launched a vicious and merciless attack against me. Praise the Lord that YAHWEH is merciful because the attack had gotten so bad that He numbed me from its sting.

Debt is financial slavery. That's how we ought to see it. Sure, we finance homes, lease cars and acquire medical bills, all in which seem justifiable, but God's plan for us does not involve us being in debt. In fact, if at all possible, you should avoid owing anyone anything. There are times when we don't have a choice but to go into debt with someone, but debt is a state that you don't want to stay in long. It's a place of transition... a place that you should only enter if you have no other route to take and a place that you exit the minute a way of escape is provided for you. There are many millionaires who would tell you that some debt is healthy debt because it serves to benefit them. Then again, there are many self-made millionaires who will warn you about debt because they've witnessed firsthand how debt has impacted (or threatened) their lives. Most millionaires are investors, investing in real estate, businesses and the like, and of course, they want a return on their investments. Additionally, many wealthy men and women don't have any liquid assets. Their money is tied up in real estate investments or business inventory. Because of this, they are what is commonly referred to as paper millionaires. What is a paper millionaire? According to investopedia.com, a paper millionaire is: *An individual who has achieved a high net worth as a result of the large total market value of the assets he or she owns. This phenomenon usually occurs when investors buy marketable securities that are later bid up to much higher prices on the open market. While this creates large amounts of "paper profit", the paper millionaire's riches usually aren't safe until these holdings are liquidated.*

Someone who is a millionaire only on paper will promote debt because more than likely, they are in debt. Understand this: There are many poor millionaires in this world (let it soak in). They are slaves to their own wealth, working hard to at least keep their money. One major financial shift in their lives could put their wealth in jeopardy and cause them to be swallowed whole by debt. They don't have millions of dollars to spend; they have millions of dollars already spent, and they are hoping to get a return on it. That's why the minute the stock market crashes, many millionaires take their own lives. The point is... anyone (poor or rich) can become a slave to debt.

There are many little-known facts about debt and they include, but are not limited to the following:

- **Debt destroys marriages-** Studies have shown that debt hinders a couple's communication, negatively impacts their sex lives and causes health complications. Because of this, more than 80% of divorced couples said that financial hardship was the culprit behind their divorces. "For I hate divorce," says the LORD, the God of Israel, "and him who covers his garment with wrong," says the LORD of hosts. "So take heed to your spirit, that you do not deal treacherously" (Malachi 2:16/ NASB).
- **Debt affects an individual's mental health-** Did you know that studies have found that debt is responsible for many mental disorders? More than twenty percent of suicides in the United States alone are linked to

debt. Can you imagine what type of mental toll (and warfare) a person has to endure to even consider taking his or her own life?
"The blessing of the LORD makes rich, and he adds no sorrow with it" (Proverbs 8:22/ ESV).

- **In America, you don't own everything you've paid for**- This includes that house you've paid off and gotten the deed to. Don't believe me? Stop paying the property taxes and watch how fast the government places a lien against your home. Truthfully, a homeowner in America is just a glorified renter. How so? Anything you have to pay to keep is not yours. Does this mean that we should stop buying homes or start buying homes abroad? No and yes. Buying homes is a great investment because it lessens the overall amount you would pay over the course of your life for a residence. It also gives you an asset that you can pass on to your children. As for buying abroad, I highly recommend doing so. Why? Because the property you purchase is actually yours if you buy it in country that does not charge property taxes. This gives you an inheritance that you can *truly* leave to your children. The average American child inherits a lot of debt from his or her parents, and many children lose their parents' homes to foreclosure. Leave them something that's truly an inheritance. (Note: Countries that do not have any property taxes include: Croatia, Monaco, Cayman Islands, Dominica, Turks and Caicos Islands, Israel, Fiji... just to name a few.)

"A good man leaves an inheritance to his children's children, but the sinner's wealth is laid up for the righteous" (Proverbs 13:22/ ESV).

- **Bad credit can ruin your day (or your life)-** Nowadays, a bad credit score could stop you from getting a decent job! It can also cause you to have to pay more money for car or home insurance. Additionally, many renters are now checking credit, and if your credit score is bad, it will be difficult for you to purchase a home at a normal interest rate. You would have to go to a high-risk lender and end up paying far more for your home than you would have if you had decent credit.

- **The average person is literally paying to fit in-** Most debt was incurred, not because the borrower needed the money, but because the borrower was simply trying to impress someone or fit in with a certain group of people. Here's the truth. We are affected by what we see and what we believe and the average human being does care what others think about him or her. Because of this, many people live to please their families and their neighbors, or at least, validate themselves to them. The large majority of debt in the United States today was incurred by individuals who simply wanted to get the approval, and sometimes, jealousy of others.

"Do not be conformed to this world, but be transformed by the renewal of your mind, that by testing you may discern what is the will of God, what is good and acceptable and perfect" (Romans 12:2/ ESV).

Regardless of what anyone tells you, debt is not your friend. Of course, spiritually speaking, it is placing you at the mercy of another human being. There are two things that you can owe a person.... one is money and the other is an apology. There are two ways to forgive a person... one is by accepting their apology and the other is by forgiving their debt (or whatever it is that they owe you). In other words, debt gives us the power to bind people, whereas, forgiveness gives us the power to free them.

Stop trying to fit in with the crowd and learn to be the unique you that you were created (by God) to be. When we try to follow the crowd, we cheapen ourselves in our attempts to fit in. Nevertheless, when we dare to stand out, even in the midst of oppositions such as jealousy and persecution, we learn just how valuable we are. At the same time, by not valuing people's unsolicited opinions about us, we are refusing to devalue ourselves just so they can reach us. This is how you get a voice that can be heard from all around the world... a voice that impacts the lives of others.

To Tithe or Not to Tithe

The church has been divided for quite some time now regarding the law of tithing. This is unfortunate because the truth is readily available for anyone to read. The problem today is that many in the church do not analyze the scriptures, nor do they ask the Lord for understanding. People don't like to study, and because of this, many have not shown themselves approved before God. Instead, the average believer chooses his or her own church without any direction from God, and then, that believer adopts that church's doctrine.

Some years ago, I went to a New Year's Eve party where I came across a pastor who spoke against tithing. His doctrine offended me, so I attempted to reason with him, but he had clearly done a lot of research about tithing and its origins. Nevertheless, I rejected the doctrine he was promoting and I reasoned within myself that his stand against tithing was the very reason he was struggling financially. At the same time, some of the things he said were powerful enough to get my attention. I could not deny that he'd done his research and he was backing his beliefs up with the Word of God. As for me, I did like most believers do. I backed up my beliefs with Malachi 3:10, but as soon as I spoke, the pastor was ready with an answer.

After I left the party, I was still faithful to the tithing doctrine. I hadn't done any research at that time because, in my mind, he had to be wrong; there was no way around it. I knew too many good, God-fearing leaders who spoke for tithing and he was the first person I'd ever heard speak against it. The basis for my belief that tithing was scriptural had nothing to do with my own study of the scriptures; it had everything to do with my respect for the leaders I'd heard teach about tithing. I had never done any research myself, nor had I prayed about it. **2 Timothy 2:15 (KJV):** Study to shew thyself approved unto God, a workman that needeth not to be ashamed, rightly dividing the word of truth.

Time went by and I started seeing more leaders posting their beliefs on social media about tithing. Many of these leaders were people I respected and knew to be men and women of God, so I decided to pray about it and do some research of my own. After all, I did not want to find myself outside of the will of God in any area of my life. I understood that if I was out of God's will financially, I would be opening my finances up for the enemy to repeatedly attack them. I went to Google and searched the following questions:
(1). Is tithing Old Testament?

(2). Is tithing scriptural?

(3). What is the origin of tithing?

These questions pulled up a lot of articles, most of them being written by people who said that tithing was Old Testament. Of course, I could not loan myself to their beliefs, so I searched an online Bible to see if I could find any mention of tithing in the New Testament. It was there, but it was mainly Jesus dealing with hypocritical Pharisees who religiously followed the Old Testament law. Jesus rebuked them because, even though they tithed faithfully, they failed to demonstrate love and mercy, which of course, is the very nature of God. **Luke 18:9-14 (KJV):** And he spake this parable unto certain which trusted in themselves that they were righteous, and despised others: Two men went up into the temple to pray; the one a Pharisee, and the other a publican. The Pharisee stood and prayed thus with himself, God, I thank thee,

that I am not as other men are,
extortioners, unjust, adulterers, or even as
this publican. I fast twice in the week, I give
tithes of all that I possess. And the
publican, standing afar off, would not lift up
so much as his eyes unto heaven, but
smote upon his breast, saying, God be
merciful to me a sinner. I tell you, this man
went down to his house justified rather
than the other: for every one that exalteth
himself shall be abased; and he that
humbleth himself shall be exalted.

Matthew 23:23 (NIV): Woe to you,
teachers of the law and Pharisees, you
hypocrites! You give a tenth of your spices--
mint, dill and cumin. But you have
neglected the more important matters of
the law--justice, mercy and faithfulness. You
should have practiced the latter, without
neglecting the former.

Luke 11:42 (ESV): But woe to you
Pharisees! For you tithe mint and rue and
every herb, and neglect justice and the love

of God. These you ought to have done, without neglecting the others.

Another notable mention of tithing in the New Testament can be found in Hebrews 7, where the order of Melchizedek was explained, and then, Jesus was compared to Melchizedek. Hebrews 7 reiterates the fact that Abraham, a righteous man, gave tithes to Melchizedek, who the Bible referred to as "priest of the Most High God." It mentioned the fact that Melchizedek had not come from the descendants of Abraham, therefore, he was not a Levite. This meant that he should ordinarily not have received tithes, but Abraham honored him by paying tithes to him.

Hebrews 7:4-6 (ESV): See how great this man was to whom Abraham the patriarch gave a tenth of the spoils! And those descendants of Levi who receive the priestly office have a commandment in the law to take tithes from the people, that is, from their brothers, though these also are descended from Abraham. But this man who does not have his descent from them received tithes from Abraham and blessed him who had the promises.

Finally, Hebrews 7 went on to further address the Levitical priesthood, which, of course, we know was established through the Mosaic law.

Hebrews 7:11-12 (ESV): See how great this man was to whom Abraham the patriarch gave a tenth of the spoils! And those descendants of Levi who receive the priestly office have a commandment in the law to take tithes from the people, that is, from their brothers, though these also are descended from Abraham. But this man who does not have his descent from them received tithes from Abraham and blessed him who had the promises.

In my research, I kept finding that the tithe

was a part of the law, but I wasn't searching for anything that supported the nonpayment of tithes; I was searching for scriptures and articles that supported paying them. After all, the belief that I was supposed to tithe was so embedded in me that I only wanted to find material that would support my beliefs. I studied the origins of tithing so that I could be ready to address the next person who spoke against it. I remembered that the main scripture used to support tithing in the New Testament church was Malachi 3:10 when the Lord was rebuking Israel and charging them to get in order for the coming of the Christ. I went back and reread the scripture, hoping to find something to support my beliefs.

Malachi 3:8-12 (ESV): Will man rob God? Yet you are robbing me. But you say, 'How have we robbed you?' In your tithes and contributions. You are cursed with a curse, for you are robbing me, the whole nation of you. Bring the full tithe into the storehouse, that there may be food in my house. And thereby put me to the test, says the Lord of hosts, if I will not open the windows of heaven for you and pour down for you a blessing until there is no more need. I will rebuke the devourer for you, so that it will not destroy the fruits of your soil, and your vine in the field shall not fail to bear, says the Lord of hosts. Then all nations will call you blessed, for you will be a land of delight, says the Lord of hosts.

After some extensive research and praying, I came to understand that the Lord used Malachi to prophesy to the Levitical priests as well as the Israelites. They'd turned away from God and had been offering sick and lame animals to God. They'd been keeping the best of the tithes for themselves. God was charging them to return to Him, and helping them understand why they had been operating under a curse. Malachi 3:10

was not a directive for the New Testament believer since we are no longer under the Mosaic Law; instead, we are now under grace.

To better understand Malachi 3, we must first understand the origin and purpose of tithing. In the book of Exodus, God commanded that every believer sanctify the firstborn of every child and animal born to them. To sanctify means to set aside or set apart. He also required that His people bring in the first fruits that sprung up from the ground.

Exodus 13:2 (KJV): Sanctify unto me all the firstborn, whatsoever opens the womb among the children of Israel, both of man and of beast: it is mine.

Of course, if we remember God's command to Cain and Abel, we will better understand the principles of giving offerings to God. Neither man was required of God to give an offering to Him (at that time), but they both did so anyhow. This was their way of showing their love and appreciation to God. Abel's offering pleased the Lord, but Cain's offering was rejected by God. Why was this? Because Cain gave an offering that came out of cursed ground. Before we give anything to God, we must make sure that it is sanctified by God so that it is acceptable to Him.

Genesis 3:17-18 (ESV): And to Adam he said, "Because you have listened to the voice of your wife and have eaten of the tree of which I commanded you, 'You shall not eat of it, 'cursed is the ground because of you; in pain you shall eat of it all the days of your life; thorns and thistles it shall bring forth for you; and you shall eat the plants of the field.

God required the firstborn of every clean animal, but Cain attempted to offer up to God a sacrifice that he'd toiled for instead of a sacrifice he'd been graced with. This, of course, wasn't tithing; the people were giving a required offering to God.

Before the Mosaic Law was established, tithing was believed to be pagan practice. Many scholars believe that when Abraham gave tithes to Melchizedek, he was simply following the customs of that time. After he gave tithes to Melchizedek, there was no other mention in the Bible in relation to Abraham giving tithes. The first literal mention of tithing as it relates to believers was found in Genesis 14:18-20 when Abraham (then Abram) gave tithes to Melchizedek.

Genesis 14:18-20 (KJV): And Melchizedek king of Salem brought forth bread and wine: and he was the priest of the most high God. And he blessed him, and said, Blessed be Abram of the most high God, possessor of heaven and earth: And blessed be the most high God, which hath delivered thine enemies into thy hand. And he gave him tithes of all.

Abraham (then Abram) did not work to earn the cattle or the grain that he'd tithed from. Instead, they were the spoils of war. There was no law that required him to give tithes to Melchizedek, but his choice to do so represented an offering of free will.

The next notable mention of tithing can be found in the book of Genesis, chapter 28. Jacob had stopped on his journey toward Haran to rest, and he had a dream. In that dream, the Lord spoke to Jacob and told him that He was going to give him and his descendants the land he was resting on. **Genesis 28:10-22 (ESV):** Jacob left Beersheba and went toward Haran. And he came to a certain place and stayed there that night, because the sun had set. Taking one of the stones of the place, he put it under his head and lay down in that place to sleep. And he dreamed, and behold, there was a ladder set up on the earth, and the top of it reached to heaven. And behold, the angels of God were ascending and descending on it! And behold, the Lord stood above it and said, "I am the Lord, the God of Abraham your father and the God of Isaac. The land on which you lie I will give to you and to your offspring. Your offspring shall be like the dust of the earth, and you shall spread abroad to the west and to the east and to the north and to the south, and in you and your offspring shall all the families of the earth be blessed. Behold, I am with you and will keep you wherever you go, and will bring you back to this land. For I will not leave you until I have done what I have promised you." Then Jacob awoke from his sleep and said, "Surely the Lord is in this place, and I did not know it." And he was afraid and said, "How awesome is this place! This is none other than the house of God, and this is the gate of heaven."

So early in the morning Jacob took the stone that he had put under his head and set it up for a pillar and poured oil on the top of it. He called the name of that place Bethel, but the name of the city was Luz at the first. Then Jacob made a vow, saying, "If God will be with me and will keep me in this way that I go, and will give me bread to eat and clothing to wear, so that I come again to my father's house in peace, then the Lord shall be my God, and this stone, which I have set up for a pillar, shall be God's house. And of all that you give me I will give a full tenth to you."

As you can see, God did not require a tithe from Jacob. Jacob's choice to give a tenth of everything God had given him was an offering of love, or better yet, a free-will offering. This, of course, was before the Mosaic Law was established.

When tithing was established under the Mosaic Law, all of Israel was required to give a tenth of their cattle and produce to the Levites. The Levites were the firstborn males from Aaron's descendants and Moses' older brother. They were the male-children who had to be sanctified, or better yet, set aside to be used by God. Levitical priests were the "go-betweens" or mediators between Israel and God. They were the ones who offered up the sacrificial offerings to God on behalf of the Jews. The offerings had to be spotless and, of course, this represented the sacrificial Lamb who would later come and die for our sins: Jesus Christ. He was His mother's firstborn son and the firstborn son of God. He was spotless and free of sin. His blood redeemed us from our sins. Additionally, it redeemed us from the curse of the law.

Levitical priests were responsible for offering up sacrifices to God, and that's why the people of God were required to bring their tithes and offerings to them. Additionally, Levitical priests received no inheritance of land, unlike everyone else. Instead, they were allowed to keep 90% of the tithes. They were required to give the other ten percent to God.

Numbers 18:21-32 (ESV): To the Levites I have given every tithe in Israel for an inheritance, in return for their service that they do, their service in the tent of meeting, so that the people of Israel do not come near the tent of meeting, lest they bear sin and die. But the Levites shall do the service of the tent of meeting, and they shall bear their iniquity. It shall be a perpetual statute throughout your generations, and among the people of Israel they shall have no inheritance. For the tithe of the people of Israel, which they present as a contribution to the Lord, I have given to the Levites for an inheritance. Therefore I have said of them that they shall have no inheritance among the people of Israel."

And the Lord spoke to Moses, saying, "Moreover, you shall speak and say to the Levites, 'When you take from the people of Israel the tithe that I have given you from them for your inheritance, then you shall present a contribution from it to the Lord, a tithe of the tithe. And your contribution shall be counted to you as though it were the grain of the threshing floor, and as the fullness of the winepress. So you shall also present a contribution to the Lord from all your tithes, which you receive from the people of Israel. And from it you shall give the Lord's contribution to Aaron the priest. Out of all the gifts to you, you shall present every contribution due to the Lord; from each its best part is to be dedicated.' Therefore you shall say to them, 'When you have offered from it the best of it, then the rest shall be counted to the Levites as produce of the threshing floor, and as produce of the winepress. And you may eat it in any place, you and your households, for it is your reward in return for your service in the tent of meeting. And you shall bear no sin by reason of it, when you have contributed the best of it. But you shall not profane the holy things of the people of Israel, lest you die.'"

So what do we say about tithes then? Tithing was indeed a part of the Mosaic Law; it was Old Testament. We are now under the law of grace and the law of love. **John 13:34-35 (ESV):** A new commandment I give to you, that you love one another: just as I have loved you, you also are to love one another. By this all people will know that you are my disciples, if you have love for one another."
Galatians 5:13-14 (ESV): For you were called to freedom, brothers. Only do not use your freedom as an opportunity for the flesh, but through love serve one another. For the whole law is fulfilled in one word:

"You shall love your neighbor as yourself."
Galatians 6:2 (ESV): Bear one another's burdens, and so fulfill the law of Christ.
Luke 10:25-28 (ESV): And behold, a lawyer stood up to put him to the test, saying, "Teacher, what shall I do to inherit eternal life?" He said to him, "What is written in the Law? How do you read it?" And he answered, "You shall love the Lord your God with all your heart and with all your soul and with all your strength and with all your mind, and your neighbor as yourself." And he said to him, "You have answered correctly; do this, and you will live."

There were three forms of tithing, each with its own purpose.
- The Levitical Tithes.
- The Tithe of the Feasts.
- The Tithe for the Poor.

Levitical Tithes
Numbers 18:21-24 (ESV): To the Levites I

have given every tithe in Israel for an inheritance, in return for their service that they do, their service in the tent of meeting, so that the people of Israel do not come near the tent of meeting, lest they bear sin and die. But the Levites shall do the service of the tent of meeting, and they shall bear their iniquity. It shall be a perpetual statute throughout your generations, and among the people of Israel they shall have no inheritance. For the tithe of the people of Israel, which they present as a contribution to the Lord, I have given to the Levites for an inheritance. Therefore I have said of them that they shall have no inheritance among the people of Israel."

As we can see, the Levitical tithe was for the Levitical priests since they were full-time ministers. In return for their service, God gave them the tithes and, of course, they had to give ten percent from the tithes they received to Him.

The Tithe of the Feasts

Deuteronomy 14:22-27 (ESV): You shall tithe all the yield of your seed that comes from the field year by year. And before the Lord your God, in the place that he will choose, to make his name dwell there, you shall eat the tithe of your grain, of your wine, and of your oil, and the firstborn of your herd and flock, that you may learn to fear the Lord your God always. And if the way is too long for you, so that you are not able to carry the tithe, when the Lord your God blesses you, because the place is too far from you, which the Lord your God chooses, to set his name there, then you shall turn it into money and bind up the money in your hand and go to the place that the Lord your God chooses and spend the money for whatever you desire—oxen or sheep or wine or strong drink, whatever your appetite craves. And you shall eat there before the Lord your God and rejoice, you and your household. And you shall not neglect the Levite who is within your towns, for he has no portion or inheritance with you.

The tithe of the feasts was for the people. It was pretty much like a fund set aside for the Jews to go on vacation.

The Tithe for the Poor

Deuteronomy 14:28-29 (ESV): At the end of every three years you shall bring out all the tithe of your produce in the same year and lay it up within your towns. And the Levite, because he has no portion or inheritance with you, and the sojourner, the fatherless, and the widow, who are within your towns, shall come and eat and be filled, that the Lord your God may bless you in all the work of your hands that you do.

The tithe for the poor was, of course, money set aside for the poor. This money was to be set aside and only used every three years.

The first tithe was for God, the second tithe was for the individual believer, and the third one was for the believer's neighbor. What does this mean for today's modern church? If the church operates under the law of tithing, it is supposed to practice every form of tithing. Jesus completed the Mosaic Law, but He did not nullify it. He simply finished it.

Does this mean we should stop giving God the first fruit of our income? No! It means we are no longer obligated to give tithes (a tenth of our earnings) because we are no longer under the Mosaic Law. Instead, our giving now comes from a place of love and not from us attempting to redeem ourselves of the sins we've committed because Christ has already bore our sins for us. The Levitical priesthood was done away with and nowadays, all believers who have

the Holy Spirit are priests of God.
Revelation 1:5-6 (ESV): To him who loves us and has freed us from our sins by his blood and made us a kingdom, priests to his God and Father, to him be glory and dominion forever and ever. Amen.

Additionally, since the Levitical priesthood was done away with, we no longer have to give a tenth of our earnings to the priests because men and women serving as five-fold leaders can now own land. They are no longer restricted to the laws that the Levitical Priests were restricted to. All the same, the people of God no longer have to stand outside of buildings created by man's hands. Nowadays, we have the Holy Spirit of God; we are the temples of the living God. This means we no longer need a priest to go before God on our behalves because Jesus, the High Priest, is now our Mediator. Finally, we no longer offer up the blood of bulls and goats because the blood of Jesus has redeemed us from the curse of the law.

The Mosaic Law was not annulled; it was completed. We no longer give because of obligation; our giving now comes from love. Our love for God and our love for our leaders should compel us to give. A person under the law of love will oftentimes feel compelled to give more than ten percent of their income to their leaders. Instead, they will give from the heart and not from a place of obligation.

Does this mean that leaders preaching the doctrine of tithes are false teachers? Absolutely not! I've met some God-fearing, holiness preaching leaders who preach tithing and will not compromise the gospel. I've also met some God-fearing, holiness preaching leaders who preach non-tithing who will not compromise the gospel. Our beliefs boil down to what we know, what we've learned and what we are required to teach. Some leaders no longer follow the doctrine of tithing, but they preach tithing because they are under fellowships where tithing is a required teaching.

Of course, it took me a long time to adjust my mind to the idea that I was tithing into the Old Testament, while attempting to live under the New Testament. I was so bound by religion that, even though I had every piece of evidence I needed to support the truth, I wanted to hold fast to what I believed. However, it was never about the money for me; it was and is about me staying in the will of God, regardless of how unpopular my stance is.

As of today, I have visited a few churches and most of them support tithing, which again, is no problem for me because, as I mentioned previously, there are some Holy Spirit filled leaders out there who preach for tithing. My stance is... I simply want to be where His Spirit is. Additionally, I have learned to give from a heart of love and follow my own convictions. I do this by asking the Lord how much I should give each time I visit His sanctuary. Whatever number He lays on my heart, that is what I give.

Whether you tithe or not is your choice. Everyone follows his or her own convictions, but I urge you to study and show yourself approved. Pray and ask the Lord for guidance in relation to every area of your life. Don't adopt a doctrine just because it's popular. Don't support a doctrine just because you support the man or woman of God promoting it. You have to get to a place in your life where you desire the truth and not just religion. A true reverence of God will cause you to yield your heart to the unpopular truth as well as the popular one. I didn't choose to stop giving; I chose to stop following the Mosaic Law, which of course, is beneficial for teaching. Christ didn't annul the law; He fulfilled it, and by doing so, He gave me a greater responsibility than what I had before. My love is now tested, stretched and challenged all the more, and the love of money can no longer exist in my heart because I can only give to one master in love. If I give to God, but my heart is in love with money, the Lord will require that I give Him enough to break that relationship with money. Of course, this figure would hurt every form of religious thinking that may have gone by undetected in my heart. You will find many millionaires in the church who God has commanded to give up the majority of their wealth. He didn't do this to hurt them; He did this to ensure that they did not fall prey to the love of money. Nevertheless, He returned and increased every penny they had given. If I give to God from a heart of love, my love for Him would compel me to not count out how much money I should give to the leaders He chooses to shepherd me. This means that I can now be a cheerful giver instead of a giver who pretends to be cheerful, all the while, worrying about the mounting bills at home. My leaders no longer have to stir my spirit up to give, and hurry up and take an offering before doubt sets back in with me. Instead, I am now in submission to the Holy Spirit who lives within me. Jesus completed the law and fulfilled His purpose on Earth, and we should all desire to live under the law of love, rather than trying to perform under the Mosaic Law.

The purpose of this chapter was to help you understand that it is necessary for you to study the Word of God. That way, you will not subject yourself to laws, cultures and practices that God is not a part of. We are no longer cursed; we are the righteousness of God through Christ Jesus. Your giving does affect your finances and that's why you should go to God for yourself to get a better understanding of what it is He requires of you. Remember, the law did not justify anyone; it condemned them, therefore, sowing into it can be summed up as sowing into the very condemnation that Jesus set us free from.

Galatians 2:15-16 (ESV): We ourselves are Jews by birth and not Gentile sinners; yet we know that a person is not justified by works of the law but through faith in Jesus Christ, so we also have believed in Christ Jesus, in order to be justified by faith in Christ and not by works of the law, because by works of the law no one will be justified. **Romans 8:1-8 (ESV):** There is therefore now no condemnation for those who are in Christ Jesus. For the law of the Spirit of life has set you free in Christ Jesus from the law of sin and death. For God has done what the law, weakened by the flesh, could not do. By sending his own Son in the likeness of sinful flesh and for sin, he condemned sin in the flesh, in order that the righteous requirement of the law might be fulfilled in us, who walk not according to the flesh but according to the Spirit. For those who live according to the flesh set their minds on the things of the flesh, but those who live according to the Spirit set their minds on the things of the Spirit. For to set the mind on the flesh is death, but to set the mind on the Spirit is life and peace. For the mind that is set on the flesh is hostile to God, for it does not submit to God's law; indeed, it cannot. Those who are in the flesh cannot please God.

Buried Talents

What is a talent? A talent is a gift that God has built into a person. It is the seed within us that contains our success. It is a spiritual currency that must be planted in the natural realm to bring forth the harvest that the spiritual realm has impregnated us with. This natural harvest is designed to build the kingdom of God in the realm of the earth. When the Bible spoke of a talent, however, it was referring to a form of currency called drachma. The drachma was a Greek coin considered to be one day's wages for a soldier or common laborer. It was 6,000 denarii, and a denarius was a Roman silver coin weighing about four grams, believed to be about the equivalent of $360,000 American dollars today (2016). What does this mean for the believer? The church should not be poor at all! A talent was one day's wages for a common soldier, but today, only twenty percent of Americans make six figures in a year's time. We've truly been robbed by our own ignorance. Every one of God's people is a millionaire, but the problem is... the wealth is locked up on the inside of us, and our lack is not a reflection of God's inability to provide for us. It is a reflection of our own ignorance and lack of a tangible relationship with God. How does Satan keep us from tapping into this wealth? By locking us into communities and families that are ignorant of his devices, ignorant of God's Word and ignorant of their own abilities. The root word of "ignorant" is "ignore", which means, that we are ignoring information that is present for the taking.

Did you know that a millionaire can be bound by the strongman of poverty? Having millions or billions of dollars does not mean that a person has the mind of

Christ. A person can be a millionaire or a billionaire and still not be successful. How so? Success isn't defined by how much money you make. Success is being able to accomplish your purpose in life while having your every need supplied. A person who has an overabundance of money is wealthy, but they aren't necessarily successful. A successful person has peace of mind, joy of heart and an immeasurable amount of love to share. At the same time, one man's measure of success is another man's measure of failure. For example, if a wealthy man leaves all of his wealth to his son, and his son never earns a penny, but instead, lives off his father's wealth, he is not a successful man. This is because he hasn't moved in life. He started at the top and spent his way downward. A rich man's top step (peak of success) is his children's bottom step (starting point).

As a young woman between the age of 18

and 22, I liked to hang out in rough neighborhoods because they were my strongholds. They were the places where I not only felt safe, but I was able to relate to others and not stand out. Whenever I went to a party, I would notice men who clearly stood out. They were clearly foreigners to the neighborhood, but they weren't too far removed from the mindset. Before long, their names and financial statuses would be known to everyone in the party. They were the children of wealthy people, but they were rebelling against high society and everything it stood for. They loved fast cars, fast girls and fast money. For many of the guys, they were failures to their dads and they felt like failures compared to their peers, but when they came to the rough side of town, they were treated like success stories. Crowds of guys would be standing near them as they lifted up the hood of their sport cars to show off their revved-up engines. In some cases, the young show-offs would dress in attire that made them stand out all the more, but in other cases, they wore clothes that represented the cultures they were visiting or the mindsets they were in. Were these guy success stories? No. They were the children of wealthy parents. Were they talented? Of course, but somehow, their parents had overlooked their own unique talents, and in their attempts to force their own personal talents or skill-sets on their children, they had lost them. You see, the neighborhoods these guys were visiting were full of talented people who didn't realize the wealth that was within them. Nobody ever showed them their worth. Nobody took the time to invest in who they were deep down on the inside. Instead, people supported their perceptions of them, so just like any lost young man, they looked for their identities in material possessions. These guys were no different than the guys in the rough areas. They didn't know who they were, so their common interests led them to one another.

All the same, there are people with little to no money who are not bound by the strongman of poverty. How so? The lack or presence of wealth does not determine whether a person is successful or not. Sometimes, a person's wealth is tied up in investments. Other times, a person's wealth is tied up in ideas that have not been birthed yet. There are even some times when a person's wealth is tied up in ideas that have been put into motion but have not yet gained their momentum. These men and women have the mind of Christ and an unyielding determination that matches their unwavering faith. Without the money in pocket, they are already successful, even though many in the world do not yet recognize them as success stories. This is because many people have been conditioned to believe that success is tied to money and money is tied to success. When individuals with this mindset are suddenly made wealthy, many of them become depressed, while others go as far as to take their own lives. This is because they believed that the highest point they could reach was to acquire monetary wealth, but once they got that wealth, they didn't have an up to look up to anymore. So, when the problems of life came upon them... problems that money could not fix, there was no vision left in them to reach for. Because of this, they felt doomed and the only direction they could see was down. In a misguided attempt to secure their names at the top, they took their own lives.

There are many millionaires in the making hiding out in ghettos, trailer parks and slums all around the world. They don't have the cash, nor do they have any liquid assets, but they have the talents they need to tap into wealth. What's keeping them from their wealthy places?

- **Many are not in their seasons.**
  With God, there is a season for
  everything. When the right season
  comes, if they are in position, they
  will enter their wealthy places.
- **Many have not yet sown the
  necessary seeds.** Believe it or not,
  many people are just one seed away
  from becoming millionaires.
- **They are connected to the wrong
  people.** God won't connect you to
  wealth if you're surrounded by the
  wrong people. This is because God
  blesses us and adds no sorrow to
  those blessings. If you are
  surrounded by the wrong people
  when you walk into your wealthy
  place, this puts your life in danger.
- **They don't have the faith (in God)
  to succeed.** Trusting God is an
  absolute must. Nevertheless, many
  people have immeasurable wealth

trapped on the inside of them, but their lack of faith has disabled them from being able to tap into that wealth. That's why God tells us to seek the kingdom of God and all His righteousness first. He said that if we did so, He would add everything else to us. When you seek the kingdom of God, you are, in the same, seeking the heart of God. Faith is simply having an intimate relationship with God to the point where you trust Him without seeing whatever it is that you're trusting Him for.

- **They don't believe in themselves.** Having faith in God is the most important thing to have, but believing in yourself is also a must. How so? If you don't trust what God has placed on the inside of you, you will trust what Satan has placed on the inside of someone else. This means that you'll be easily led astray by wolves in sheep's clothing.

- **They are surrounded by people who don't believe in them.** There are millions, if not billions, of children and adults who are extremely (and uniquely) talented, but they've placed their confidence in the people around them. People who are familiar with you oftentimes have trouble seeing you as a success story, so instead of celebrating and sowing into you, they'll criticize and question you. That's why a millionaire's journey to wealth is oftentimes a lonely one. He wakes up one day and can count the number of active relationships he has with friends and family on one hand.

- **They haven't made the right connections yet-** Plants need water to grow. Sometimes, God will place what you need to grow on the inside of another person. He does this so that you won't take the glory for yourself, but will instead, recognize that He has gifted you and He divinely connected you to the right person or the right people.

- **They are afraid of wealth and success-** One of the most surprising facts that is rarely shared is that more than 50% of people in poverty are terrified of wealth. Many simply want enough money to live comfortably off, but the idea of being wealthy is scary to them. The reason for this is that most people are afraid of what they do not know or understand. Many people in poverty think that wealthy people are rich and lonely snobs with bank accounts bigger than their hearts. They are bound by perceptions and those perceptions limit them in their dealings. The same goes for most rich people who've never been poor.

- **They are currently in sin**- I'm sure you've probably heard the cliché: *God don't bless mess.* That statement couldn't be any truer. God extends grace to us, but when we are bound by sin, we are untrustworthy servants. Because of this, a wealthy backslider would likely never return to God because of his wealth.
- **They refuse to come outside of their comfort zones-** Comfort zones are the graveyards where many talents are buried.

Every pointer above can be summed up this way: They keep burying their talents.
The Bible tells a wonderful story of three men who were given talents. Each man was given a talent in accordance with his own ability. Of course, the word "ability" references an individual's skill, knowledge, expertise or gifting. *(Note: This is why it is very important not to limit one's self to a*

single skill-set.)

In the story, the three men were all servants of the same master. The Bible tells us that their master "entrusted" (put trust in) each man in accordance with his own ability. This should help us to understand the heart of God. He entrusts us with wealth when we are able to handle it and when we are trustworthy servants of His.

After the master gave the talents to each of his servants, he demonstrated his trust by leaving them. We can all attest to the fact that none of us like to have our bosses breathing down our necks, especially if we have been given any measure of authority. As human beings, we want to prove ourselves trustworthy, so a manager must allow the associates under his direction to manage whatever it is that he has entrusted them with. How they handle the authority they are given will determine their ranking or their job security.

Luke 12:48 (ESV): Everyone to whom much was given, of him much will be required, and from him to whom they entrusted much, they will demand the more.

The servant who was given one talent further proved that he was not trustworthy. He buried the talent, instead of trying to increase it. In other words, he did not love or respect his master. He simply wanted to return to him the talent that had been given to him. Furthermore, he went on to do something we see a lot of people doing today. Instead of telling the master the good news of what he'd done, he gave his master his talent back along with an excuse. This is how the strongman of poverty works! Understand this: God has placed one or more talents in every person breathing on the face of this earth. Let's define poverty this way: *Poverty is the presence of a buried talent.* The enemy has convinced most of the people on the face of this earth that their talents are nothing but hobbies or things they like to do in their spare time. He's convinced them to put more confidence in their skills (learned abilities) than they do in the very talents that were handed to them by God. So, they bury their talents and sharpen their skill sets. They depend on this world's pyramid-shaped system (government) more than they trust in the sovereign God who reigns over every system, power, principality and demon in heaven, earth and hell.

Another avenue that many take is applying kingdom principles to a product or service. Believe it or not, kingdom principles will work regardless of where they are applied or who applies them. There are many secular millionaires and billionaires who've acquired their success by applying kingdom principles to their businesses or careers. They have unearthed buried talents, invested in them and doubled them. Talents are like cash; they can be used regardless of how they were acquired or where they will be spent. A twenty dollar bill found on the ground can be spent the same way that a twenty dollar bill that was earned can be spent. All the same, a woman who has a beautiful voice and sings demonic music can sell her music just like a woman who has a beautiful voice and sings for the Lord.

Romans 11:29 (KJV): For the gifts and calling of God are without repentance.

The talents that God has invested in us, or better yet, entrusted us with, all have within them the ability to acquire wealth. Talents are nothing but seeds, but if we never plant those seeds, we can never expect a harvest from them. All the same, there is a difference between planting a seed and burying one. When you plant a seed, you plant it in expectation. You understand the life-bearing nature of that seed, so you sow it at the depth it needs to be sown into the ground it needs to be sown in. You then nurture that seed by giving it water and attention so that it can grow up. You would prune away anything that threatens the life and growth of that seed.

Burying a seed, on the other hand, means that you throw it into any ground with no expectation because we only bury that which is dead. Additionally, we bury what is dead at a far greater depth than we plant what we expect to live. This is to ensure that the dead thing does not resurface and the stench of the dead thing is kept contained. Dead things don't grow; they break down. People don't bury living things unless they intend to kill them. Many people bury their talents, go to church, and then, chant religious cliches over the graveyards in which they've buried their talents, hoping to conjure up blessings. This is because they do not understand the principles of sowing (planting) and reaping (harvesting). Many misguided or misinformed leaders have taught their sheep to invest into their (the leaders') talents rather than investing in what God has placed on the inside of them. Of course, this doesn't necessarily mean they are hell-bound leaders; it simply means they lack wisdom, knowledge and understanding in certain areas.

Sure, we ought to invest in our churches and sow into our leaders, but we must also remember that God holds each man accountable for himself. This means that we cannot bury talents and blame our disobedience on our pastors. God requires that we all have individual relationships with Him outside of corporate settings. When we are tuned in to the heart of God, He will show us what He has invested in us, and then, He will tell us how to double our talents, therefore, doubling our harvest.

Philippians 2:12-13 (ESV): Therefore, my beloved, as you have always obeyed, so now, not only as in my presence but much more in my absence, work out your own salvation with fear and trembling, for it is God who works in you, both to will and to work for his good pleasure.

Lastly, our talents won't always be understood by everyone, including our religious leaders. Many people bury their talents because they are surrounded by the wrong people. The wrong people will almost always give you the wrong advice, seasoned with a good nugget here and there. People with limited thinking will always seek to place limitations on the people in their reach, and that's why it is necessary to get out of some people's reach. For example, when I started off in business some years ago, I would occasionally have people reaching out to me who were not personal friends of mine, but they were on some of my social media networking pages. In other words, I was within their reach. Anyhow, they began to question me about creating Bishop Seals, ministry logos and the like. They wanted to know the origin of a Bishop's Seal, and when I told them, they still proceeded to demonize the graphics. Even though they had no knowledge of its history, they spoke reproachfully of them because of their lack of understanding. Of course, I started ignoring their messages, and a few of them did not like being ignored, so they tried to demonize me. I deleted them from my social networking pages because they were clearly people who did not need to reach me. You see, some people will never let you go to any place mentally, socially, financially or spiritually if they do not understand where you're going. At the same time, if you connect to people who do not understand you, they will try to reel you back into a place that they do understand. In other words, if allowed, they would make their realities your reality.

As God continued to increase my talents and I began to write books, start new businesses and do new things, people who shouldn't have had any way to reach me began to reach out to me all the more. They weren't criticizing any specific work that I was doing anymore; instead, the new criticism was about the fact that I was doing a lot of things (web design, graphic design, book publishing, editing, writing books, photography, blogging, etc.). To my surprise, I've had a few people (less than a handful, thankfully) tell me that I was trying to do too much. Nevertheless, I didn't listen to them, and anytime you refuse to accept a person's opinion of you, they will distance themselves from you, but not before sharing their unsolicited opinion about you. Because I refused to listen to people, but instead, kept my ears tuned in to the voice of God, the Lord blessed me with many businesses and He blessed me to write many books. Like most people, when I first started off, I did question myself and I went before God several times about some of the things people had said to me, but God would so lovingly rebuke me with one question: *I gave the assignment to you. How do you expect them to understand it, seeing, as it is, that they were not equipped or assigned for your journey?*

There are talents in all of us, and the more we tap in to them, the more the enemy will use people to reel us back into the prisons and coffins he's designed for us. Understand that the more you do for God, the more persecution you will have to endure because persecution is always indicative of ignorance. People persecute what they do not understand. In other words, the chain Satan uses to bind God's people is the lack of knowledge, and if you allow them to, they will use the chains that they are bound with to bind you. Just like hurt people hurt people, bound people bind people. Bound people come in all shapes, colors, ethnicity and religious ranks. If you respect one over the other, Satan will use the very thing (or person) you respect to bind you.

The Culture of Poverty

Poverty is a state of mind. Let's place emphasis on the word "state." When we speak of a state in the noun sense, we think of one of the fifty states that make up North America. Of course, a state in the noun sense, is a physical place that can be entered, lived in and exited. The same goes for mental states but they aren't physical places; they are mindsets, or better yet, mental places. Poverty is a state of the mind; it is a place where wealth is allowed just as long as it does not have wisdom attached to it. It is a state that can be entered, lived in and exited. Nevertheless, because of a lack of knowledge, many people don't know how to move out of poverty and into a better way of thinking.

Just like a natural state, a mental or spiritual

state has neighborhoods, economic classes, cultures and subcultures. With poverty, there are many cultures and subcultures; for example, if you've grown up in a crime-ridden area, you'll know that not everyone in those areas can relate to one another. In one house lives a woman who's pretty much given up on herself. She doesn't think she can be anything outside of what she currently is. Because of this, she parties a lot, hangs around a rough crowd, loves getting tattoos on her body and she's promiscuous. In another house lives a woman who's aspiring to be a Certified Nurse's Assistant. Sure, Certified Nurse Assistants don't earn much money, nor is the CNA field one that promises any sort of upward movement career-wise, but for her, going to school is a big deal. The last fifteen generations of women in her family didn't go to school. Instead, her family has relied on the government to provide for them for more than a century. She is the first woman in her family to step foot into a college, so going to school to do anything is a huge step in the right direction.

Both women live a few hundred feet from one another and both women have their own group of friends (cliques) that they hang around. Let's call the tattoo-loving, complacent woman Margie and the soon-to-be CNA Delores.

Margie doesn't like Delores. As a matter of fact, she thinks that Delores is an egotistical wannabe who needs someone to humble her. Delores isn't too fond of Margie. She thinks that Margie is an angry, self-mutilating woman who simply hasn't received her prison uniform yet. Both women hang around people who are like themselves, and anytime they see one another, they do not speak. Why is this. Both women submit to different subcultures under the culture of poverty.

The truth is... Delores is trying to break away from the chains that have bound her family, and in some neighborhoods, this would put Delores in danger. Again, it depends on the subculture that is commonly practiced in the area. In some impoverished areas, most of the residents are trying to better themselves by going to college, and even better, by trying to get to know God on a more intimate level. In other areas, it is rare to see an individual with ambition, and because of this, should one rise up and it becomes public knowledge that the individual is seeking to better him or herself, that individual would likely be threatened, mocked, intimidated, persecuted and ostracized altogether. In many cases, that individual would be physically attacked by a person or a group claiming that the individual has said something or behaved in some sort of way that's disrespectful to them. Of course, this wouldn't be true. The attack would simply be the offender or offenders' attempt to "humble" the person they feel has gotten too high-minded.

Again, one thing you have to know is that everyone who lives in an impoverished neighborhood is not in subjection to the strongman of poverty. Some people are just in bad areas because God is using those areas as training grounds for their ministries. Some of today's most renown celebrities were raised in impoverished areas by parents who were bound by the strongman of poverty. Through their familiar connections (family, friends and neighbors), they have been subjected to every demon associated with poverty and almost every mindset under the culture and subcultures of poverty. Nevertheless, they themselves resisted poverty's strongman and dared to stand out.

People who resist poverty in poverty-stricken areas are often ridiculed by their peers, family, and worst of all, their own parents. You see, poverty is a state of mind that their parents live in, and in order for them to relate to their parents, they will have to live in and embrace their parents' mindsets. Because they are different (in mind), there is a lot of indifference between them. They can't agree with one another because they are living in the same house, raised in the same conditions, part of the same family, but they are living under different authorities. The parents are in submission to Mammon, but they are in submission to God. Such individuals have had to grow up with siblings who mocked, humiliated and attacked them repeatedly simply because they were different. They didn't fit in because God called them out the moment they were conceived in their mothers' wombs.

Amos 3:3 (KJV): Can two walk together, except they be agreed?

Jeremiah 1:5 (NIV): Before I formed you in the womb I knew you, before you were born I set you apart; I appointed you as a prophet to the nations.

Google defines "subculture" as: *a cultural group within a larger culture, often having beliefs or interests at variance with those of the larger culture.* A few examples of subcultures include hip hop (which of course, is a lifestyle), Goth (witchcraft culture) and bikers (people who form groups or gangs to travel together). Nevertheless, every subculture does not have labels to identify with. Instead, society as a whole tends to label the subcultures they feel have the greatest impact on their own lives, often disregarding the smaller subcultures. Of course, this is why our society is crumbling. Sometimes, it's the scrawny man with the ax who makes the greatest impact on the tree.

There are subcultures in the church as well. It goes without saying that God never intended for culture to get into the church, but it has, and because of this, there are religious cultures and religious subcultures. Many of these cultures and subcultures are governed by the principality of Mammon. For example, we know that God loves a cheerful giver, meaning, He wants people to give from their hearts. He wants people to give because they trust Him and they love Him. He does not want anyone giving out of fear or obligation.

1 John 4:8 (ESV): There is no fear in love, but perfect love casts out fear. For fear has to do with punishment, and whoever fears has not been perfected in love.

A religious leader under the principality of Mammon will use fear tactics and manipulation in his or her attempt to persuade the congregation into giving more. These tactics include, but are not limited to:

- Telling the congregation that they are going to hell for not giving.
- Promoting and recognizing the members (and non-members) who are faithful in their giving. Sometimes, they recognize people who are not faithful givers, but they do give large sums of money occasionally.
- Giving favorable treatment to the members who give the most. This includes having them seated in the best seats in the sanctuary or going to dinner with them.
- Telling people that the attacks on their lives are because they were not faithful givers.
- Telling stories to the congregation of others who were not givers or were not faithful givers. These stories always end in the non-givers' fall or death.

- Telling people that God said (or has commanded) that they give a certain amount of money, even though they (the members) themselves have not heard God say this.

Of course, we know that God breaks our ungodly relationships with money by having us to give, and sometimes, what He tells us to give offends our religious thinking. Nevertheless, He does not use fear to build faith. He uses the Word to build faith, therefore, a person who is not a faithful giver doesn't need to be intimidated, mocked, threatened or made to feel inferior to the faithful givers; they simply need more Word. At the same time, they need to be set free from the government of poverty so they can submit to God's authority. This, in itself, takes time because God will use the leader to systematically, but lovingly, tear down their old mindsets so that He can give them the mind of Christ. When this happens, they receive the understanding they will need to not only be givers, but they will get the understanding that they need to become cheerful and faithful givers. Not only does it require patience on their part to arrive at a new mindset, but the leader(s) God has appointed to shepherd them must also be patient enough to let God bring the increase out of them. After all, cultures and traditions are the hardest strongholds to break... especially when they are grafted in religiously.

1 Corinthians 3:7 (KJV): So then neither is he that planteth any thing, neither he that watereth; but God that giveth the increase.

Cultural thinking in the church is nothing more than worldly thinking that somehow found its way into the church and was never corrected. Instead, the people who were submitted to that mindset were likely promoted in the church, and this gave them (and their demons) the authority they needed to influence small and/or large numbers of people. Believe it or not, cultural thinking can become an epidemic in and outside of the church. For example, the punk rock culture is a demonic culture that has found its way into many churches. Anytime someone who is not delivered from the familiar spirits that have been leading, tormenting and seducing them becomes the leader of a church's praise and worship team, that person will change the sound that's being released in that church. They will use the instrumental tracks of worldly music, change the lyrics of those songs and have the choir singing them. No longer will the choir worship the Lord in Spirit and in Truth. True worship music will slowly become a thing of the past as it is replaced by sounds from hell. Some of those churches' members will flee for their lives as culture begins to infiltrate their churches. They will be labeled as religious souls who aren't willing to change with the times. The ones who stay behind will find themselves being pulled into the darkness of their new governments, where demons disguised as angels of light will begin to take authority over them.

People submitted to poverty's culture are submitted to the opinions and expectations of their peers. In our society, it takes a lot of courage to stand out... especially in communities where standing out could cost you your life.

One thing about the strongman behind poverty is that it causes the person bound by it to restrict themselves to only that in which they can see. That's why it's essential for a person bound by poverty to see someone who looks like him or herself on the other side of the cultural lines of poverty. One of the greatest threats to the strongman of poverty, outside of the Word of God (of course) is experience. If a man who's escaped poverty and became a success story were to return to the community he grew up in and invest wisdom, knowledge and understanding into some of the young men in that community, he would make a huge impact. Undoubtedly, at least one of the young men who hears his testimony will escape, not just the community that has him bound, but the mindset that imprisoned him to that community in the first place. Nevertheless, many people are afraid to return to their old communities. They know that many of the residents who do not want to change are territorial, and therefore, see any and every outsider as a threat to their communities. Because of this, many former residents of that community would put their lives at risk to return to them. Thankfully, this hasn't stopped many people who've escaped poverty from returning to their old neighborhoods, however.

Satan doesn't want the people bound by him to see any form of light because this would give them hope. To ensure that there is no unity, he draws more lines of division and uses the ignorance of every culture to keep people from uniting and learning from one another. He uses race, creed, religion, economic status and just about every difference imaginable to promote division. He then divides every race, creed, religion, economic status, etc. into cultures and subcultures. Basically, it's like taking a credit card statement and ripping it in half, and then, ripping the two halves into smaller pieces. You'd continue ripping the paper until it was too small to be ripped. By doing so, you make it almost impossible for anyone to put the statement back together and read the information on it. That's why there are many subcultures. Satan is ripping God's people apart by what they can see, and keeping them ignorant of their true enemy... the one they cannot see.

Nowadays, there are many cultures, subcultures and divisive lines within subcultures. Inside poverty's culture, you will find many people who would make a great impact on this nation and the world if they were simply shown the way out. Of course, they would first have to divorce poverty and every mindset associated with poverty before they can make an impact that doesn't divide the people all the more. It has happened and God will continue to raise up soldiers who are not afraid of Satan... people who understand that even the government of Mammon is subject to the kingdom of God. These people will boldly walk into lands infested with devils and they will start setting God's people free. They will be the Moses and the Harriet Tubmans of their generations, and nothing shall by any means harm them. The enemy struck them on their feet (direction), but they will strike him on his head (authority), thus, removing his authority over many people. Poverty is a culture, whether we want to admit to it or not, but the great thing about culture is.... it can be entered, lived in and exited. Anyone who wants to be free can be free; they just have to be bold enough to fight the enemy who has them bound. The great news is that Christ has already defeated Satan, so the fight is already fixed. They simply need to accept Christ as their Lord and Savior, and then, get to know Him. The more you know Christ, the more you'll know your rights in Christ Jesus. The more you know your rights, the less power the enemy and all of his sublets have over you.

__Generational Poverty__

"Social and economic deprivation during childhood and adolescence can have a lasting effect on individuals, making it difficult for children who grow up in low-income families to escape poverty when they become adults. Because the negative effects of deprivation on human development tend to accumulate, individuals with greater exposure to poverty during childhood are likely to have more difficulty escaping poverty as adults" (Ref: National Center for Children in Poverty).

As I mentioned earlier, my Dad taught me almost everything I needed to know to be broke and stay broke. In my earlier years, I took what I was taught and ruined my credit. Over time, having bad credit and mounting bills became a huge burden on me, but I had spent my life surrounded by people with the same issues. So, it goes without saying that being broken and burdened was my version of normal, even though it didn't feel good.

As time went on, I began to meet people outside of the people I grew up around and I was introduced to new ways of thinking and reasoning. I was amazed to come across people who were passionate about paying their bills on time. I watched in awe as some people drove cars that were not in the best shape simply because they wanted to balance their budgets, save money and plan for a better future. In the mental universe I was from, this concept was foreign. I couldn't understand how someone could have money sitting in their bank account adding up. Why wasn't the idea of shopping as overwhelming to them as it was to me? How could they walk through the mall and come out with the one thing they'd gone in there for without buying anything else? How could they not take advantage of the amazing clearance sales that were going on? My questions were many because the idea of saving for a future that probably didn't exist was a foreign concept to me. I didn't know it at the time, but I was one of the lowest slaves on Mammon's totem pole; I was a slave assigned to work in the state of poverty. I didn't like my reality, and when you don't like your reality, you won't like yourself. I didn't know anything about generational poverty. Truthfully, I lacked the knowledge of poverty itself and I think this is true for most people in poverty.

Generational poverty isn't a generational curse; it is more so inherited thinking. Our parents always pass something on to us. When they pass wealth to us, that wealth is referred to as an inheritance. When they pass debt to us, that debt is a burden and the mindset behind that debt serves as a generational stronghold. The Bible tells us that a good man leaves an inheritance for his children and his children's children (see Proverbs 13:22).

Imagine that generational debt had a face, an identity and a personality. It has been the financial adviser for your family for hundreds, if not, thousands of years. It hasn't taught them how to become success stories. Instead, it taught them how to stay poor. Understand this: God has placed in us the ability to become millionaires and success stories on our own. The seeds are already within us. We don't need a success coach, someone to believe in us or a multi-million dollar investor to be successful in life. Sure, all of these people can be a great help to us, but the truth is, we don't need them. We simply need to hearken to the voice of the Holy Spirit and He will serve as our financial adviser, big-money investor and our greatest supporter. He will teach us everything we need to become the success stories we were designed to be. However, generational doubt comes into the picture and teaches us how to be poor. Being poor is something that we have to be taught because we are seed-bearing children of God. All we need is to be obedient children of God and sow the seeds that are in us into fertile ground and watch them yield their harvests. Believe it or not, success is a part of our instinctive nature; it is who we are as a people. Satan knows this, but he also knows that parents pass their thinking on to their children. How could he affect, not just one generation, but generations to come? By simply contaminating our thinking with false doctrine and promoting the lack of knowledge. The seeds in us aren't just our abilities and talents; they are our supernatural abilities to birth heaven in the realm of the earth. Know this: We are anointed to win, but we were perverted to fail.

To be anointed is to be supernaturally endowed with power. To be perverted means to be naturally or spiritually corrupted by sin. We are born pregnant with power; we are born pregnant with success, but to be perverted means to operate contrary to our God-given designs. It means that we abort God's blessings in us in our attempts to birth out something we feel is better suited for us. In perversion, we hand over our God-given power to the enemy and submit to the authority of the one whose belief system we have joined ourselves to.

When our parents gave birth to us, they gave us the supernatural ability to succeed, but if their thinking patterns weren't lined up with the Word of God, they taught us how to fail repeatedly. If we didn't give ourselves completely to God and embrace new mindsets, we would pass along those thinking patterns to our children. They would then pass them to their children, who would, in return, pass them to their children. This is generational poverty, and of course, this serves as a generational curse.

What exactly is a curse? The word "curse" is one of the most misunderstood words in the Bible. For this reason, many dictionaries (big and small) have redefined the word in accordance with our limited understanding. The word "curse" is not God's intention to inflict harm or to punish His people. The word "curse" is synonymous (biblically speaking) with the word "perverse." God created us to operate and think a certain way. When our thinking and/or our ways are not in line with how God created us, we have been perverted, or better yet, altered by sin. Perversion can be generational or self-inflicted. The word "curse" is more so God's reaction to perversion, or better yet, sin. He can't bless it, so He has to curse it, meaning, He has to place judgment upon it. When God denounces something, He also renounces it. This means that He simply removes His blessing from it. The words "denounce" and "renounce" are similar. However, the differences are that the word "denounce" involves making a decree or a judgment public, whereas, the word "renounce" means to reject something. When God removes His blessing from something, He is pretty much saying that He wants nothing to do with the fruit of whatsoever it is that He rejected because that thing is rooted in sin, and will therefore, yield fruit after its own nature. In other words, God publicly rejects some "thing" or some "one" by declaring that thing or that person wicked, or better yet, godless. Of course, godless means to be without God. This means that whatever

God has withdrawn Himself from has the responsibility of producing its own harvest. When Adam and Eve sinned, God removed His blessings from the ground, which meant that Adam had to work to get a harvest from it. Before their fall, Adam and Eve did not have to lift a finger; they were able to live a blessed life simply because of whose they were. When God removed His blessings from Cain, He did not remove His love from Cain because Cain had sown a wicked seed by killing his brother, Abel. Instead, God allowed Cain to reap what he had sown. God said that any man who killed Cain would suffer vengeance seven times over, and He put a mark on Cain to serve as a warning to anyone who saw him that he was not to be touched. What happened here? God extended grace to Cain, but of course, He was not going to bless Cain's mess. Because of how He created us, God knew that whatsoever we were (sinner or saint), we would produce seeds (children and works) after our own kind.

Generational poverty is pretty much a mentality that God is not a part of. It goes without saying that if God is not a part of it, Satan is a part of it. Satan is the author of lies, therefore making him a liar, or the father of all lies. This means that lies aren't just words we speak that are not true, but lies are doctrines that are contrary to the Word of God. A person under the strongman of poverty is full of demonic doctrine, which mentally places that person in a godless state of mind. Remember to see the word "state" in this context as a place similar to Georgia, Florida, Nevada, etc. It is a location; a place that can be entered, lived in and exited. Wrongful thinking is not a physical place; it is a mental place that represents the spiritual government that many are in submission to. Generational poverty means that one generation after the other has submitted to a state of mind that God has denounced. By doing so, they have repeatedly rejected God's blessings, which means, they have to toil for their food. Of course, in the United States alone, there are many people who do not work... people who have the ability to work, but choose to depend on the government for their substance. Are they impoverished? Yes. But how is it that they are able to eat and have a place to stay, given the fact that 2 Thessalonians 3:10 reads, *"For even when we were with you, we would give you this command: If anyone is not willing to work, let him not eat?"* Review the posted scripture again. You'll notice that the Apostle Paul said that the commandment was for the church of Thessalonica to stop feeding people who refused to work. This didn't mean that the church was to stop feeding the widow, the orphans and those who were unable to work. It meant that every able-bodied person should have continued operating in the system of sowing and reaping. Additionally, it meant that there were some people in the church of Thessalonica who were unwilling to work and the rest of the church was allowing these people to eat freely. In other words, there were some people taking advantage of the system that was in place within that church.

Able-bodied adults who refuse to work are dead weight to anyone who takes the charge of carrying them financially. That's why the United States government is designed around a godless system that keeps it in debt. Someone will carry the debt of a person who refuses to work, because we (the people) are consumers, meaning, we need something to consume, and of course, whatever it is that we consume has a price tag, or better yet, a debt tied to it. To get whatever it is that we need, we must exchange what we do have (the ability to work) for it. When a person is not working, someone else has to work and earn those things on that person's behalf, and even though the government tries to shift the bulk of that responsibility to the middle class, it has affected every class. In an attempt to make the rich richer, many who head up the United States governmental system forgot to do the math involved. They didn't realize that debt was a recurring fee that would shift from one hand to the other until it was paid off. It's similar to a torch that keeps getting passed around. They simply thought that the debt would shift to the middle class, and therefore, the middle class would serve as a roof for the poor, providing shelter, food and necessities to those who need it. At the same time, they would provide a cushion for the rich to fall on. They didn't realize that the system they organized was an ungodly set-up that would have a boomerang and a toppling effect. When the national debt became too heavy for the middle class to balance, it caused a domino effect. Consequently, many who were considered middle class fell beneath the poverty line. This increased unemployment, which of course, decreased overall spending. After a while, the upper class had to start taking on some of the responsibility of those who refused to work. The point is that poverty affects everyone, but knowledge distributed is wealth distributed.

Generational poverty is a parent's legacy for his or her children. Parents who pass poverty on to their children hand them a mental passport to lack. They teach their children to forfeit the blessings of God, and then, spend their lives pursuing those blessings through worldly avenues.

Can generational poverty be escaped? Of course it can. I escaped poverty, and I didn't have to go the worldly route to do so. Christ called me out of poverty and He took me on a very lengthy journey designed to help me find myself once again. I met a version of me that I didn't know existed and I'm still being introduced to many facets of her personality to this very day.

A few things to expect when you start your journey out of poverty is:

- **God may separate you from most, if not all of your family.** When God called me out of poverty, I thought I could bring my family and friends with me. I was wrong. Over time, I watched as one relationship after the other came to an end, or at least, transitioned from being a close-knit relationship to a casual one. You have to be okay with walking alone for a few seasons. Of course, this won't feel good to you, and there will be times when loneliness will try to haunt you, but you're not leaving your family behind. The truth is... you are showing them that there is a way out.

- **Making friends won't be so easy anymore.** As you acquire more knowledge from God, you will find that the number of people who are able to relate to you will decrease. In order for someone to relate to you, they must be relative to you. Not a relative of yours, but they must be relative to you. This means they must have some comparative experiences. Anytime you find yourself hanging around people who aren't able to sharpen you, you will be considered the dull friend who's always trying to sharpen them. This means you'll be considered the weirdo of the group.
- **Some of the people you respect the most will mock, criticize or distance themselves from you.**

One thing you'll learn about a journey is that any one who is not allowed to take that journey with you will get offended. This is normal. All the same, anytime we reverence or respect another person, that person takes it upon himself or herself to become our unofficial life coach. When this happens, the person who fashions himself or herself as your teacher will always see you as "their" student, meaning, you are not expected (by them) to go any further than they have gone. When you start stepping outside of their knowledge's limitations, they will become offended and attempt to reel you back in. If you refuse to get back in the place or mindset they believe is best suited for you, they may ridicule you, distance themselves from you and demonize you. Even though this behavior is not good, it is to be expected.

- **Frustration is commonplace in the beginning of your transition out of poverty.** The reason frustration is so common for people in transition is because we feel at ease when we are in our comfort zones, but anytime we are being shifted out of those comfort zones, we become frustrated. Frustration is not an indication that you've failed; it is the evidence of you being in a new place spiritually.

Poverty in the Sanctuary

My businesses primarily deals with ministries; I create ministerial seals, logos and crests for ministries. I also create websites, design flyers, produce video commercials, publish books, etc. My company brands ministries, and since its launch, we have worked with thousands of ministries from around the world. The experience has not only been humbling, but it has been educational. When I started off in business, I had a glorious perception of anyone who had a religious title. I knew that there were false apostles, teachers, prophets, evangelists and pastors out there, but it was too foreign of a concept for me to grasp. It was hard for me to fathom the idea that anyone would purposely dishonor God. Additionally, I had to learn that some people are truly a part of God's five-fold setup, but their minds have not completely undergone a full renewing. Because of this, the first year being in business was very humbling for me. I found myself frustrated, even angry at times because I had been manipulated or had endured quite a few manipulation attempts and I'd grown tired of the games. I simply wanted to have a problem-free business, but of course, I had a lot of growing up to do as an entrepreneur. I would often find myself on the phone calling back customers who verbally ordered a seal, but after sending them a copy of the design, I never heard back from them. Of course, I no longer operate this way. I require upfront payment these days.

Anyhow, I became very distrusting, and this distrust echoed from my website's frequently asked questions page. I posted some of the offensive questions that I received, and then, I answered those questions as if I was speaking to a thief posing as a pastor. It didn't take me long to find myself again and realize that my issues came from my lack of rules and order. Once I implemented new guidelines, additional fees, and restrictions, my experiences improved and I started getting more orderly customers. What happened? My lack of order, guidelines and additional fees attracted frugal people who liked disorder, hated rules and loved delegating. This time in my life taught me to stop looking at titles and start inspecting fruit.

When I launched my publishing company, the frugal minds came out again because my prices were far less than most self-publishers. I would find myself on the phone for lengthy amounts of time listening to someone go on and on about the book God had given him or her. It would always start off with the person complimenting me, and then, the caller would shift the tone of the conversation and begin to give me the lengthiest version of his or her personal biography possible. The story would encapsulate some of the many great deeds the person had done, including sowing huge amounts of money into people and/ or organizations. *Sometimes, I'd even get an unsolicited prophecy.* Nevertheless, the story would always end with the individual explaining why he or she had no money to pay for my services. The caller would always be waiting for the funds to come in. There were times when those calls had gone on for over an hour. Again, this was my fault because I didn't have any rules in place. After the callers finished their testimonies, they would hold the line to see if I was going to offer them some sort of discount for wasting my time, or better yet, offer my services for free. Some people would directly ask me for free services, while others, would try to manipulate them out of me. For the ones who were indirect, I would simply tell them that their testimonies were great. After that, I would proceed to give them my pricing. I would end my speech by telling the caller that when he or she had the funds, they could give me a call back so that I can start the order. Of course, this response did not sit well with many people. Some people would rush off the phone, others would delete me from their social media pages, while others, would finally take the direct approach. I would always explain to the callers that God would never give them an assignment without giving them the provision to complete that assignment. I recognized the mindsets immediately. I'd grown up around those mindsets. They were what is commonly referred to as poverty mindsets. It goes without saying that the large majority of my customers were not and are not like this. However, I would occasionally get someone who was bound by the poverty mindset. This didn't mean that they were false leaders (even though some were), but for many, it simply meant that they needed to fully denounce Mammon and all of his works once and for all.

Poverty is a prevalent mindset in the church, spanning from the leadership (in some churches) to the congregation. Of course, God does not want His people operating under demonic influence because this represents the lack of a sober, God-trusting mind. Sometimes, as believers, we trust God in certain areas of our lives, but we do not trust Him in other areas. The main area people have trouble believing God in is their finances. When you don't trust God in the area of your finances, you will turn to other devices to make or save money. When you don't trust God with your finances, you will become manipulative in your attempts to get whatever it is that you want or need. Anytime a person does not have faith in the financial arena, that person will struggle with their finances, which, of course, will cause them to become even more manipulative. He or she will look to others to fund their visions and supply their needs, and this dependency is ungodly. That's why some leaders get angry at the members who do not tithe, give offerings or do not give the amount of tithes and offerings they believe the members have the ability to give. The problem oftentimes is that the leader is depending on that money to pay bills, whether it's the church's bills or his or her own personal bills. Of course, the congregation should be diligent givers, but leaders should never depend on the sheep to give. They should always depend on God and He will turn the hearts of the people He wants to use to sow into their ministries. There will be some disobedient members, and there will be some obedient ones, nevertheless, God will always make sure that any sanctuary under His government suffers no lack or need. When lack is present, it's because doubt is present. When lack is present, it is sometimes indicative of the presence of an ungodly rule or government in place. Lack is almost always a representation or manifestation of our faith or lack thereof.

God's children are citizens of prosperity, but many have migrated to poverty using the lack of knowledge, procrastination and/or fear as their passports. Many have walked away from their own promised lands to follow up behind religiousness, rather than holiness. Religiousness promotes the false teaching that God does not want anyone in leadership to be wealthy, and if they are, they must rid themselves of the wealth to enter heaven. Such teaching is misguided and unbiblical. Religiousness teaches that God's desire for His people is that we

264

submit ourselves to impoverished lifestyles, all the while, chanting religious cliches in an attempt to get God to at least pay our electricity bills. Religiousness teaches that it is God's will that we live on the edge, barely being able to pay our bills each month. This is all untrue. God's desire is that we have a heart for the kingdom of God and the people of God. His plans for us involves us seeking the kingdom of God and all His righteousness first. From there, He said He would add everything else to us. This means that God doesn't want us pursuing wealth, fame or anything. He wants us to seek Him, and then, watch Him bring every thing we want to fruition. When we seek wealth, we step outside the will of God and into a state of mind that's governed by Mammon. From there, we'll become inundated with imaginations of fame, success, prosperity and whatever soulish fantasy our flesh can conjure up. Instead of casting these imaginations down

like the Word tells us to, we would easily
find ourselves being led astray by our own
lusts. The enemy won't tell us that we're
lost. As a matter of fact, he will encourage
us to go to church and keep chanting
religious adages. You see, we'll decree and
declare the right thing in the wrong place,
hoping that God won't see the state of our
hearts but will instead, focus on our crafty
words and authoritative tones. Again, when
our hearts aren't right with God, we will
easily become manipulative, even
attempting to manipulate the all-knowing
YAHWEH!

Poverty has become commonplace in many
Christian sanctuaries because of lack of
knowledge. We must understand that it is
not God's will that we live in lack. God's
vision for the church is that we are first and
foremost in His will, focused primarily on
His heart and endowed with every blessing
heaven has to offer. It is His will that we be

the government because dominion was given to the believer. It is not His will that the wicked rule His people because the wicked will always create laws that mirror the laws established under Satan's government. We can't bring the world into the church and expect God to rule alongside Mammon. The principality of Mammon is ungodly and it has no place in God's government! We must eradicate poverty from the church, but to do this, we must denounce and renounce Mammon. Of course, this would be a huge challenge for the ones who are seated on the wealthy side of Mammon's rule. Truthfully, the greatest opposition to evicting Mammon has come and will come from church folks who love what Mammon has done for them! Nevertheless, we (the true church) have been given authority over **all** the powers of darkness. This includes the darkness that is seated in the sanctuary.

Overcoming Poverty's Strongman

Poverty is a strongman, or better yet, a stronghold. The way to overcome a strongman is to become the strongman in your home. You can either be bound by a spirit or you can bind that spirit. Of course, there are demonic spirits in operation, but you must first bind the principality in your life before you can uproot the strongman. **Mark 3:27 (ESV):** But no one can enter a strong man's house and plunder his goods, unless he first binds the strong man. Then indeed he may plunder his house.

To understand the strongman of poverty, you must first understand the strength of the strongman. To understand the strongman's strength, you must first recognize your own weaknesses. A strongman can only be a stronghold in an area of your life where your faith is weak. For example, some people are fearful of the opinions of others. This is a stronghold brought on by the haughty spirit behind pride. Pride encourages selfishness (selfish ambition, self-pity and self-conceit). By doing so, it provokes its captives to value (or fear) the opinions of others, believing that people have within them the power to promote or demote them. This haughty spirit blinds its captives and causes them to become near-sighted, which means that they look at every person and every opportunity from a selfish place. Everything they do and say must benefit them, even when they are doing charitable works. For example, a man with a haughty spirit will want pictures of himself giving food to the homeless, so that he can post those pictures online. Such individuals love the praise of man because they've become their very own idols. People under the siege of this stronghold are easily offended because they are always guarding themselves against perceived threats. For example, a captive woman may hear a group of women laughing and think they're laughing at her, even though the women don't know her, aren't looking at her and haven't done anything to make her feel that way. Because she's always defending herself, she's always offended at anyone she thinks is against her.

The strength of the strongman in your life can be broken and Satan's hold on you can be destroyed, but you must first realize that you're bound, and then, fill yourself up with the Word of God. When you allow the Word into your heart and you believe the Word, it becomes a sword. It is then that you can take that sword and sever every ungodly principality, tear down every demonic stronghold and cause to flee every devil that's in operation in your life.

Again, a strongman exercises its strength in your weakest areas. That's why it's important for you to identify your areas of weakness, and study scriptures that speak to those areas. For example, if your weakness is spending, you should study Proverbs 21:20 and Proverbs 6:6-8. If your weakness is withholding, you should study scriptures that teach about the spirit of fear; after all, people who have trouble releasing money are bound by fear. A few scriptures you should memorize are Philippians 4:6-7, Proverbs 12:25 and Psalm 42:5.

How did I overcome Mammon and all of its strongholds? It took me almost a decade to get free (counting from the time I gave my life to Christ). The reason it took a long time for me was because poverty had been rooted so deeply in my family that I needed to be broken time and time again so that

God could pull that foolish thinking out of me. The first thing God did was to send me to a church that some would consider to be a prosperity church. I thank God for that church because it was there that God not only used my pastor to lead me to salvation, but He also used him to speak to the lack mindset I had. God used him to disturb the soil and introduce me to a new mindset. Of course, it took me a long time to fully embrace that mindset, but the woman I was when I walked into that church was not the same woman who walked out of it. That's why I'm not against prosperity teachings. I understand that God speaks to and through us all, and sometimes, He uses one person to teach a particular subject, but he will use a different person to teach on another subject. My pastor spoke on many things including holiness, forgiveness and uprooting old (non-beneficial) mentalities, but he also taught a lot about overcoming lack and lack mindsets.

After I moved to Germany, I was no longer able to visit the church God had planted me in, but the Lord continued to speak to me. I made it a point to read my Bible and pray daily. I made it a point to have an actual relationship with God that did not involve religious babbling or excuses. I broke before God many times, crying out to Him about the condition of my heart and asking Him to set me free. And every time He introduced me to a new mindset, I embraced it. Sometimes, I'd resist it at first, but once I realized that God was bringing me out of my old thinking, I let Him have His way.

Another thing was being willing to travel to other countries. My family is from Mississippi and the large majority of them have never traveled outside of the country. I went against my family and decided to travel abroad. Now, my reasoning wasn't right (my second husband lived abroad), but traveling to another country introduced me to new mindsets and it put to rest many of the foolish perceptions that once kept me bound.

Lastly, God used the people in my life to demonstrate lifestyles that were foreign to me. For example, one of my friends) who also spent her life bound by the strongman of poverty) was going through a divorce. She'd moved back to Mississippi and she wanted to make sure that she didn't have to rely on her family for help, so she would take her income tax check and pay her rent for six months at a time. She would also take what was left of her check and pay her car note and car insurance for six months. She went back to school to be a social worker, so she was also receiving a school check. Anytime she received that check, she would pay off her rent for another six months. Even when she was jobless, she lacked for nothing. She did rely on the government temporarily, but she used financial assistance the way it was supposed to be used- as a transitioning tool. After she received her Bachelor's degree, she went back and got her Master's degree. From her, I learned to throw loose money at debt and to pay off monthly utilities with earnings. I also learned to put money away.

Roger's (my ex-husband) frugal ways were the sparks behind many of our arguments when we first moved in together. As I mentioned earlier, his motto was if we didn't have the cash for it, we weren't going to have it. That included cars, furniture and every other big ticket item you can think of. The only thing Roger would consider buying on credit was a house, and he was leery about that. I didn't become frugal like Roger, but I did become wiser with my money. After years of not being harassed by bill-collectors, I found peace in not owing anyone anything. Again, once Roger and I divorced, I logged on to a credit reporting site to check my credit, and I was pleasantly surprised to see that all of the items on my credit report had fallen off of it. I was (and am) debt free for the first time in my life. I'd gone more than seven years without applying for any line of credit because I no longer saw debt as an option or a blessing. I saw debt for what it was: bondage. I had gotten a taste of freedom, and after that, there was no going back to the bondage God had delivered me from.

If poverty is the authority in your home, you have to denounce it, renounce it, take authority over it and decapitate it. When you remove the head (authority), the body (works) cannot function. How did poverty root itself in your life? Was it generational or learned? If it was generational, denounce poverty for as far back as you know your family was in poverty. Denounce it up to seven generations. If it was learned behavior, it has to be unlearned. Either way, you will need to fill up on the Word of God and learn to manage your finances with a kingdom mindset. Understand that there are a set of beliefs that have to be torn down and this won't be a comfortable process. When God changes your mind, He shifts you outside of your comfort zone, and then, He guides you to a new heart and a new mind. From there, He propels you into your destiny. You can't manage new things with old thinking.

Below are 20 tips to overcoming poverty.

1. **You have rights. You better know them or lose your stuff!** Satan knows your rights, and that's why he goes out of his way to ensure that you don't know your rights. He

knows that if you understand what belongs to you and how to get it, you'll stop following his lies and you'll start tapping into the wealth God has placed on the inside of you.

2. **Denounce, renounce and repent of the debt you've acquired.** Understand that true repentance means that you are turning your heart back to God's way of doing things, rather than following the path you've been treading.

3. **Be the creative you that you were designed to be.** Stop allowing fear to bind you and start allowing faith to free you. Just do whatever God lays on your heart to do. You will not fail at what God has designed you to do unless you fail to do it.

4. **You have to be a rookie before you're a pro!** One of the biggest problems with the church is that we want to skip the learning process and

become overnight professionals and overnight success stories. That's not how things work with God.

Everything you start off in, you start off in as a babe (starter), and then, you level up until you've grown up in it. If you don't give up, you will be an expert in whatsoever it is that God has assigned you to do.

5. **Resist the temptation to spend.** Know that there is a difference between spending and sowing. Money is a seed that only grows when its sowed, but money spent has already produced a harvest.

6. **Forgive others.** Forgiveness isn't just choosing to forgive someone for their sins or offenses against you. You also have to forgive people of their debts.

7. **Pay off any debt you owe.** Sometimes, another man's forgiveness is in your hands, or better

yet, in your pocket. If you owe money to someone, pay them back! At the same time, please remember that you are a slave to whomever you owe money to.

8. **Purposely stay out of debt.** You don't need a credit card, nor do you need any luxuries you can't afford to buy with cash. Think of it this way. You can either go a few years of not being able to afford everything you want and have no debt or you can go into debt, get the stuff you want and spend your life trying to get out of it.

9. **Stop rejecting knowledge.** People reach out to me a lot and ask me to pray for them in the area of their finances, but when I hand them the knowledge they need to set themselves free, they reject it. They don't want new knowledge; they want wealth. Remember, Solomon asked for wisdom and God blessed

him with immense wealth. I've noticed that when I respond to people who ask for prayer regarding their finances and I tell them to seek new wisdom, knowledge and understanding, they will go on and on about how much money they've tithed, sowed and how they've obeyed God in their giving. I normally respond one more time and tell them where to find wealth, but 99% of the time, they don't want knowledge; they want someone else to pray for them because they feel as if God is no longer answering their prayers. They didn't realize that God sometimes answers His people through His people and He does not always throw money at our problems. Sometimes, He hands us a shovel and calls us to dig into the deep to unearth those talents we've buried.

10. **You need new friends!** Stop feeling

indebted to old friends and let God change your circle. Once God places you around people who are not in debt, people who manage their finances with the heart of God, you just may learn new ways to manage your money.

11. **Stop following the crowd and think like a millionaire or a billionaire.** Understand that people who've acquired their wealth through faith have a mindset that sets them apart from the rest. The millionaire and billionaire statuses are labels that we give them to identify them, but there is a label that they are wearing in the realm of the spirit that sets them apart from the rest as well. They don't follow crowds, trends or traditions and you shouldn't either.

12. **Start saving money now.** Look at your finances and pay attention to what and who you've been sowing in.

Change the direction you send your finances in, and over time, you'll notice a change in what manifests in your life.

13. **Stop being a consumer and start being a producer.** Consumers consume, but producers produce, or better yet, create wealth. What are your talents? If you don't know, the answer is just a prayer away. When God reveals your talents to you, He has just revealed your spiritual account number to you. Now, all you need is your pin number (faith) and an ATM (obedient heart) to access it.

14. **Go to some building wealth seminars and buy books on building wealth.** You need new knowledge to go into new places. The average person refuses to pick up a book because they don't want to invest the time, money or energy into getting the information in the

book.

15. **Stop chasing free stuff.** One of the characteristics of a person in poverty is to chase free stuff. Stop! People will never give away valuable things without getting something they feel is more valuable in return, including your time.

16. **You have to be okay with standing out, otherwise, you won't come out of poverty.** Wealthy people are peculiar; impoverished people are familiar. Stop trying to fit in and learn to boldly stand out in Christ Jesus.

17. **Stop trying to make amends with a family that God has delivered you from.** I understand that you have your family's blood, but Jesus redeemed you from that family with His blood. If they don't want to serve the Lord, or they want to serve Him the wrong way, you will more than

likely have to distance yourself from them.

18. **Be who you are designed to be and not who you are expected to be.** This is the reason that God calls us from among people who bind us with their expectations. Sometimes, the calls on our lives are so big that they can be intimidating, and we need supportive people around us to help us launch into the deep. Be who God designed you to be, even if it offends the people who thought you should be something else.

19. **Change the channel and station or that mess will change your beliefs!** Anything that changes your mind, changes your life; that's why it is never a wise idea to invest your time in watching television shows or listening to music that offends God. Watch shows that teach you how to build or manage wealth. For

286

example, learning about the property market is a great idea and a great investment.

20. **Get your passport and go out of the country whenever you can afford to.** A cruise is not expensive if you take it in the right months, for example, March and April are inexpensive months to take cruises. Get up and do something different. Visit new nations and learn new things.

Remember this: It's the familiar stuff that's been binding you. You need new friends, new surroundings, a new mind and a new heart to come out of poverty.

Matthew 9:17 (NLT): And no one puts new wine into old wineskins. For the old skins would burst from the pressure, spilling the wine and ruining the skins. New wine is stored in new wineskins so that both are preserved.

The tips above show how to deal with the natural side of poverty, but understand that there is a spiritual side that must be dealt with as well. You have to rise up against the devil that's been rising up against you. Poverty is like cancer. It has to be cursed at the roots, otherwise, it'll come back.

2 Corinthians 10:4-5 (KJV): For the weapons of our warfare are not carnal, but mighty through God to the pulling down of strongholds; casting down arguments, and every high thing that exalts itself against the knowledge of God, and bringing into captivity every thought to the obedience of Christ.

Below are seven tips to tearing down every strongman of poverty in your home as well as generations to come.

1. **Pray down and bind the principality of Baal.** Understand that Baal is the devil behind the system. Pagans believe him to be the

god of fertility; the one who causes the earth to yield its fruit. This ungodly system is not only demonic, but it is a system that is destroying this world and many churches. Repent for allowing this principality to have authority in your life, and then denounce and renounce it.

2. **Pray down and bind the principality of Mammon.** Some people believe that Baal and Mammon are the same. They believe that Mammon is simply one of Baal's personalities, but in truth, they are not the same, even though they do work collectively. Mammon is believed to be the god of possession. He is believed to be the distributor of wealth, and guess what? If you submit to the principality of wealth, he will be the devil of wealth or poverty in your life, and he will rob you of far more than he gives to you.

Repent for allowing this principality to have authority in your life, and then denounce and renounce it.

3. **Pray down and break every generational demon, stronghold, power and principality that's in operation in your life.** You have to pray them down, bind them, and then, cast them down. How do you do this? By first repenting to God for allowing any demonic authority to be in operation in your life. After that, you denounce and renounce those principalities and devils by name. Call them out all. Even the ones behind lust, destruction and premature death. Bind them. Speak to the warring angels God has assigned to you and command them to arrest every unclean spirit, power and principality that's been in operation in your life. Tell the angels where to cast those evil ones.

Understand that we have the power to bind and loose in the realm of the earth. Angels follow the Word; they will not follow your words. That's why you have to use your God-given abilities and bind everything that's unlike God and command that the angels cast those wicked spirits into the abyss and bind them there until the day of judgment. This is warfare at its best. You are an officer of God's law. Know this: You're not only fighting against a foe that's already defeated, but you are arresting illegal devils and destroying their illegal operations in your life and the realm of the earth.

4. **Throw away all of your idols.** This includes things you've gotten through deception, manipulation, fornication and every form of sin imaginable. (Keep the kids, of course. God can redeem them.) And

don't give the idols away or sell them. Understand that you should never bind another person with what's been binding you. Purge your home of the Buddha statues and every idol that's been decorating your home, all the while, opening up doors to the demonic in your life. Ask the Lord to reveal what needs to be destroyed and He will.

5. **Cleanse your home and your life.** Go through your house with some anointed oil (blessed by a true man or woman of God) and decree and declare that the Devil, all of his workers and all of his works are no longer allowed in your home. Place the oil on every door and window in your home, and seal them shut to the Devil with the blood of Jesus.

6. **Understand that Satan is not omnipresent; he can only be in one place at one time.** What does this

mean for you? Sometimes, we try to bind Satan (before his time) without binding the actual devils that are attacking us. Just like God assigns angels to us, the demonic realm has authorities that assign devils to us. You need to know what devils are attacking you, attaching themselves to you or influencing you before you are able to effectively bind them.

7. **Repeat the steps above when necessary.** Warfare is rarely a one-time thing. You have to be more determined to be and stay free than the devils in your life are determined to keep you bound.

Understand that when you bind a devil, another like devil will oftentimes come after you. This is a direct attack against your faith. For example, if you bind the devil of lust, another devil of lust will come after you. Just as Satan isn't omnipresent, demons aren't omnipresent. This means that there is not one big collective devil of lust that comes across billions of people at one time. There are many lust devils illegally on the face of the earth. After you've bound a devil, the same type of devil comes after you because demons don't want you to believe that you are powerful enough to bind them. A person who's been struggling with lust, for example, will question why they are still struggling after they've bound the devils in their lives. After that, they will start to believe that they aren't powerful or faithful enough to be or remain free. Sometimes, people will even believe that God is angry with them, and that's how the enemy keeps them bound. Of course, this is not true; it's just the enemy's way of making sure that the person who has been bound stays bound. Do you remember how hard it was for Pharaoh to release the people of God, regardless of what he witnessed God do and regardless of what he lost trying to hold on to them? The enemy of your life was in Pharaoh, and he's just as determined to keep you in bondage as Pharaoh was to keep the Israelites. The Israelites served under Pharaoh's rule for 430 years. A generation of a man is the age of that man when his first child was born. In biblical times, the average man had his first child at 40 years old, which meant that Israel was in bondage for a little over ten generations. How many generations of your family has Satan kept in bondage? The point is that the enemy is the most persistent stalker you'll ever face. To get free is one challenge, but to stay free is another one. You have to persistently and consistently bind every devil sent your way until the demonic kingdom realizes its suffering too many casualties in its attempt to keep you.

Prayer

Lord, I repent of all of my sins, both known

and unknown, and I ask for Your forgiveness. Lord, I ask that You cover my body, spirit and soul with the blood of Jesus and let Your hand be upon me from on high. Lord, through the power of Your Holy Spirit, I decree and declare that Jesus Christ is Lord over my life. Lord, I repent of the sins of my ancestors and I uproot, cancel out and destroy every generational stronghold, curse, witchcraft, sorcery and familiar spirit that's been in operation in my life and the lives of my children. You said in Matthew 16:9 that whatever I bind on earth is bound in heaven and whatever I loose on earth is loosed in Heaven. Lord, I denounce Mammon; I denounce Baal, and I denounce every unclean spirit, power, and principality that's been operating as the authority of my life, and I give You back Your throne in my heart. Lord, tear down the principalities of Baal and Mammon in my life and the lives of my children. Let their falls be heard from around the world so that Your name will be glorified. Let them not rise again in my life, but instead, I exercise the power and authority given to me through Christ Jesus in Luke 10:19 to tread on serpents and scorpions, and over all the power of the enemy. Lord, let the words I'm about to speak manifest in heaven and in earth even as I begin to speak them. I bind every unclean spirit, power, principality and evil in my life, and I loose the warring angels of YAHWEH to arrest those evils and cast them into the abyss until the day of judgment. I plead the blood of Jesus over myself, my family, my home, my possessions and everything You have assigned to my life. Lord, glorify Your name in my life. If I am required to sow a seed to break the spirit of lack, Lord, show me where to sow that seed. Let me sow it with a joyful heart so that You will accept my offering. Open my eyes to see any and everything in my home and life that serves as a demonic portal so that I may rid my life of it. Lord, drive away every friend, family member or person who is being used by the enemy as a hindrance, spy or a threat in my life. I repent of every ungodly relationship I've been in and I commit to serving You with my body, spirit and soul. Lord, keep me in Your will and do not allow the enemy to have any authority in my life. I dedicate everything that I am and all that I have to You. I denounce poverty and break its chains over my mind and soul. Lord, let me be free and stay free but let this all be for the glory of Your name. In Jesus name, I ask these things. *Amen.*

Passport to Prosperity

The following scriptures will help you to understand your rights as a child of the Most High God. The enemy kept you and your family in bondage for hundreds, and maybe, thousands of years. He made you a citizen of sin, but through the power of God, that citizenship can be revoked if you denounce and repent of it. Let the following scriptures not only serve as your passport back to prosperity, but let them serve as your super-naturalization process back to prosperity.

What Opens the Door for Poverty

Proverbs 28:13 (NLT): People who conceal their sins will not prosper, but if they confess and turn from them, they will receive mercy.

Proverbs 10:4 (ESV): A slack hand causes poverty, but the hand of the diligent makes rich.

Proverbs 21:17 (ESV): Whoever loves pleasure will be a poor man; he who loves wine and oil will not be rich.

Defend the Poor

Proverbs 31:8 (ESV): Open your mouth for the mute, for the rights of all who are destitute.

Psalm 82:3-4 (KJV): Defend the poor and fatherless: do justice to the afflicted and needy. Deliver the poor and needy: rid them out of the hand of the wicked.

Be Careful How You Treat the Poor

Proverbs 14:31 (ESV): Whoever oppresses a poor man insults his Maker, but he who is generous to the needy honors him.

Proverbs 22:22-23 (ESV): Do not rob the poor, because he is poor, or crush the afflicted at the gate, for the Lord will plead their cause and rob of life those who rob them.

Psalm 72:3-4 (ESV): Let the mountains bear prosperity for the people, and the hills, in righteousness! May he defend the cause of the poor of the people, give deliverance to the children of the needy, and crush the oppressor!

1 John 3:17 (KJV/ 2000): But whoever has this world's goods, and sees his brother have need, and shuts up his heart of compassion from him, how dwells the love of God in him?

Watch Your Associations

Psalm 1:1-3 (ESV): Blessed is the man who walks not in the counsel of the wicked, nor stands in the way of sinners, nor sits in the seat of scoffers; but his delight is in the law of the Lord, and on his law he meditates day and night.
He is like a tree planted by streams of water that yields its fruit in its season, and its leaf does not wither. In all that he does, he prospers.

Proverbs 18:20 (ESV): Whoever walks with the wise becomes wise, but the companion of fools will suffer harm.

Proverbs 23:20-21 (NASB): Do not be with heavy drinkers of wine, *or* with gluttonous eaters of meat; for the heavy drinker and the glutton will come to poverty, and drowsiness will clothe *one* with rags.

James 4:4 (ESV): You adulterous people! Do you not know that friendship with the world is enmity with God? Therefore whoever wishes to be a friend of the world makes himself an enemy of God.

Matthew 10:34-39 (ESV): Do not think that I have come to bring peace to the earth. I have not come to bring peace, but a sword. For I have come to set a man against his father, and a daughter against her mother, and a daughter-in-law against her mother-in-law. And a person's enemies will be those of his own household. Whoever loves father or mother more than me is not worthy of me, and whoever loves son or daughter more than me is not worthy of me. And whoever does not take his cross and follow me is not worthy of me. Whoever finds his life will lose it, and whoever loses his life for my sake will find it.

Encouragement for the Poor

Psalm 113:5-8 (AKJV): Who is like to the LORD our God, who dwells on high, Who humbles himself to behold the things that are in heaven, and in the earth! He raises up the poor out of the dust, and lifts the needy out of the dunghill; that he may set him with princes, even with the princes of his people.

Pay Back Your Creditors

Proverbs 3:27-28 (ESV): Withhold not good from them to whom it is due, when it is in the power of thine hand to do it. Say not unto thy neighbour, Go, and come again, and to morrow I will give; when thou hast it by thee.

Romans 13:7 (ESV): Pay to all what is owed to them: taxes to whom taxes are owed, revenue to whom revenue is owed, respect to whom respect is owed, honor to whom honor is owed.

Be Generous in Your Giving

Proverbs 11:25 (NIV): A generous person will prosper; whoever refreshes others will be refreshed.

Proverbs 19:17 (ESV): Whoever is generous to the poor lends to the LORD, and he will repay him for his deed.

Proverbs 28:27 (NIV): Those who give to the poor will lack nothing, but those who close their eyes to them receive many curses.

Deuteronomy 15:10 (NIV): Give generously to them and do so without a grudging heart; then because of this the Lord your God will bless you in all your work and in everything you put your hand to. There will always be poor people in the land. Therefore I command you to be openhanded toward your fellow Israelites who are poor and needy in your land.

Stop Stealing and Work

Ephesians 4:28 (ESV): Let the thief no longer steal, but rather let him labor, doing honest work with his own hands, so that he may have something to share with anyone in need.

Psalm 62:10 (ESV): Put no trust in extortion; set no vain hopes on robbery; if riches increase, set not your heart on them.

Ezekiel 33:15 (KJV): If the wicked restore the pledge, give again that he had robbed, walk in the statutes of life, without committing iniquity; he shall surely live, he shall not die.

Serve God, Not Wealth

Proverbs 23:4-5 (KJV/ 2000): Labor not to be rich: cease from your own wisdom. Will you set your eyes upon that which is not? For riches certainly make themselves wings; they fly away as an eagle toward heaven.

Matthew 6:33 (ESV): But seek first the kingdom of God and his righteousness, and all these things will be added to you.

1 Timothy 6:10 (NIV): For the love of money is a root of all kinds of evil. Some people, eager for money, have wandered from the faith and pierced themselves with many griefs.

Luke 16:13 (KJV): No servant can serve two masters: for either he will hate the one, and love the other; or else he will hold to the one, and despise the other. Ye cannot serve God and mammon.

Let Holiness be Your Standard

Psalm 92:12-15 (NIV): The righteous will flourish like a palm tree, they will grow like a cedar of Lebanon; planted in the house of the LORD, they will flourish in the courts of our God. They will still bear fruit in old age, they will stay fresh and green, proclaiming, "The LORD is upright; he is my Rock, and there is no wickedness in him."

Proverbs 10:24 (ESV): What the wicked dreads will come upon him, but the desire of the righteous will be granted.

Proverbs 15:6 (ESV): In the house of the righteous there is much treasure, but trouble befalls the income of the wicked.

Just Ask

1 John 5:14-15 (ISV): And this is the confidence that we have in him: if we ask for anything according to his will, he listens to us. And if we know that he listens to our requests, we can be sure that we have what we ask him for.

James 4:2 (ESV): You desire and do not have, so you murder. You covet and cannot obtain, so you fight and quarrel. You do not have, because you do not ask.

Seek Wisdom

Proverbs 8:12-21 (ESV): I, wisdom, dwell with prudence, and I find knowledge and discretion. The fear of the Lord is hatred of evil. Pride and arrogance and the way of evil and perverted speech I hate. I have counsel and sound wisdom; I have insight; I have strength. By me kings reign, and rulers decree what is just; by me princes rule, and nobles, all who govern justly. I love those who love me, and those who seek me diligently find me. Riches and

honor are with me, enduring wealth and
righteousness. My fruit is better than gold,
even fine gold, and my yield than choice
silver. I walk in the way of righteousness,
in the paths of justice, granting an
inheritance to those who love me,
and filling their treasuries.

Trust in the Lord

Psalm 23:1 (ESV): The Lord is my
shepherd; I shall not want.

Psalms 37:3-4 (ISV): Trust in the LORD and
do good. Dwell in the land and feed on
faithfulness. Delight yourself in the LORD,
and he will give you the desires of your
heart.

Matthew 6:31 (NIV): And why do you
worry about clothes? See how the flowers
of the field grow. They do not labor or spin.
Yet I tell you that not even Solomon in all

his splendor was dressed like one of these. If that is how God clothes the grass of the field, which is here today and tomorrow is thrown into the fire, will he not much more clothe you—you of little faith? So do not worry, saying, 'What shall we eat?' or 'What shall we drink?' or 'What shall we wear?' For the pagans run after all these things, and your heavenly Father knows that you need them. But seek first his kingdom and his righteousness, and all these things will be given to you as well. Therefore do not worry about tomorrow, for tomorrow will worry about itself. Each day has enough trouble of its own.

Philippians 4:19 (KJV): But my God shall supply all your need according to his riches in glory by Christ Jesus.

Jeremiah 29:11 (NIV): "'For I know the plans I have for you," declares the LORD, "plans to prosper you and not to harm you, plans to give you hope and a future."

www.ingramcontent.com/pod-product-compliance
Lightning Source LLC
LaVergne TN
LVHW051622080426
835511LV00016B/2115